challenge, if we accept it, he holds, may revitalize our higher education. He places the Program in the broad context of institutional analysis and social theory, showing also how it is addressed to such questions as the relation of college to university, of wisdom to understanding, of the individual to society.

The book is in two parts, the first of which explores the possibilities suggested by the Berkeley experiment. The second part contains progress reports on the Program, reviews points of difficulty in realizing its initial conception, and explains modifications. Of interest to educators, sociologists, and philosophers, the work is of great importance to other segments of society as well, and to the public at large.

Joseph Tussman, Professor of Philosophy at the University of California, has been Director of the Experimental Collegiate Program at Berkeley since its beginning four years ago. He is the author also of *Obligation and the Body Politic*.

EXPERIMENT AT BERKELEY

EXPERIMENT AT BERKELEY

JOSEPH TUSSMAN

NEW YORK
OXFORD UNIVERSITY PRESS
LONDON   1969   TORONTO

Copyright © 1969 by Oxford University Press, Inc.
Library of Congress Catalogue Card Number: 77-75117
Printed in the United States of America

"I owe a cock to Aesculapius; will you remember to pay the debt?"

These, the last words of Socrates, remind the disciple of the unpaid debt to the source of healing. I have remembered them often during the past three years. Alexander Meiklejohn was my teacher, and the creation of the Experimental Program at Berkeley was—from my point of view—a simple act of discipleship.

Preface

The Experimental Program was conceived as an attempt to reincarnate the spirit and principles of The Experimental College. That college, founded by Meiklejohn at the University of Wisconsin in the 1920's, had a brilliant but brief life. It was only a memory when I was an undergraduate at Wisconsin, a legend, an educational Paradise Lost. I have always regretted that I missed it, and several decades of university teaching strengthened my belief that it offered the solution to the central problems of undergraduate education.

A concrete proposal was developed in the spring of 1964, and preliminary discussions had begun when, in the fall of 1964, the Free Speech Movement burst upon the world. This coincidence has supported the assumption that the Experimental Program is a child of the student movement; but the child does not, in any important way, resemble its putative parent. It is undoubtedly the case that the depth of student unrest and disaffection shook the complacency of the faculty and made it more receptive to drastic innovation. It is quite possible that without the prevailing sense of urgency and crisis the program would not have been authorized—at least not without considerable delay. Student unrest was, in this way, involved in the establishment of the program. The spirit of the program, however, with its completely required faculty-determined curriculum and structure is utterly alien to the spirit of "student-initiated" programs which involve students in the creation and planning of courses in which they are interested, or which, in one way or another, turn them loose to educate themselves.

During the three years the program has been in operation the world has experienced the eruption of student discontent in contagious and striking form, and everywhere there is anxious concern over how to deal with it. Are there "rights" we have failed to recognize? Are there legitimate demands that must be met? Is it an irrational storm we must try to ride out? Can we anticipate and prevent? Will minor concessions do? Or do we need fundamental reform not only of the educational institution but of society as well? Is the inherited conception of the university—whatever it may be—no longer appropriate, and must we, therefore, reshape it to a new conception of the relation of thought to action, understanding to involvement, university to society?

The Experimental Program has had its own internal struggles in its attempt to establish a radically different mode of educational life. It is not easy, under the best of circumstances, to change deeply rooted habits. But the program does not, for good or ill, exist as an island in midst of a calm sea. We had an educational idea and we were trying to carry it out. It is so fundamental a departure from the current educational pattern that most of the current educational controversy and agitation seems altogether superficial and irrelevant. Arguments about how to improve courses sound quite unreal and remote when you have simply abolished "the course" altogether. We recognize that people are still taking and giving courses. They have our sympathy, but we cannot regard their quarrels, their politics, their participatory gestures, their ad hoc concessions and innovations as very important. Why get excited about educational battles with insignificant educational stakes? When all the dust has settled things will look very much the same. Only some names will have been changed to confuse the innocent. The Experimental Program goes deeper and reduces current battle cries to triviality.

So, regarding its terms as beside the point, we stand outside the mainstream of current controversy. Student dissatisfaction with his college education is real and justified, but the demand for student participation in educational administration is a futile and misguided remedy. The faculty is right in trying to retain its educational authority, but its exercise of that authority within the habit of the course structure amounts, at the lower-division liberal arts level, to a feeble joke. On behalf of the student we oppose faculty practice; on behalf of education, we refuse to defer to student inclination or power. In the politics of education, our alliances are precarious.

We have worked during the past three years in complete freedom. The administration has been generous in its support and has imposed no restrictions upon us. At no point have we had to accommodate our educational judgment to supposed institutional, administrative, or political necessities. No one has interfered. The student culture has been generally sympathetic and supportive, even though the scale and complexity of the program make it seem, to some, at best a token remedy and not a massive solution to a massive problem. The faculty, which with some misgivings authorized the program, has been tolerant and even sympathetic. Much of its opposition based on misunderstanding has disappeared. The opposition based on understanding is yet to be reckoned with.

J. T.

Berkeley
December, 1968

Contents

Introduction

The campus may well emerge in the modern world as the successor to the marketplace, the cathedral, the factory, the financial district—as the pivotal social institution. That the campus is in turmoil is, in fact, a sign of its vitality. We are fighting about its constitutional structures, and the stakes are high.

The most significant conflict on the modern campus is not the most dramatic one. It is not between students and administration, or faculty and administration, or faculty and students; it is the subtle conflict between the university and the college. It is a peculiarly internal conflict between two tendencies within the same company of men, two purposes, two functions.

The university is the academic community organized for the pursuit of knowledge. It is arrayed under the familiar departmental banners and moves against the unknown on all fronts. Its victories have transformed the world.

The university is a collection of highly trained specialists who work with skill, persistence, and devotion. Its success is beyond question, but it pays the price of its success. The price is specialization, and it supports two unsympathetic jibes: the individual specialized scholar may find that, as with Oedipus, the pursuit of knowledge leads to impairment of vision; and, the community of scholars, speaking its special tongues, has suffered the fate of Babel.

The men who are the university are also, however, the men who are the college. But the liberal arts college is a different enterprise. It does not assault or extend the frontiers of knowledge. It has a different mission. It cultivates human understanding. The mind of the person, not the body of knowledge, is its central concern. This, I am sure, is the heart of the matter. I hope it is clear as it stands, because I despair of explaining it. Knowledge is related to understanding, but understanding is not another subject which can be taught. Wisdom can escape the expert; there are learned fools. Folklore and dark sayings, but I will rest on that for the time being. The university for multiplicity and knowledge; the college for unity and understanding.

The college is everywhere in retreat, fighting a dispirited rearguard action against the triumphant university. The upper-division, dominated by departmental cognitive interests, has become, in spirit, a preparatory run at the graduate school, increasingly professional. Only the lower-division remains outside the departmental fold—invaded, neglected, exploited, misused. It is there that the college must make its stand.

The cast of characters—students, faculty, administration—is standard but sometimes misunderstood, so a few cautionary remarks are in order.

First, "students" are not "scholars." This is not a complaint. It is a fact, and not even a deplorable one. It has nothing to do with intelligence or the capacity to learn. Some students will, of course, become scholars, just as some will become dentists. But it is a mistake to think of "training scholars" as the same thing, in principle, as "teaching students." The American college student is simply a normal American who has behaved well in high school and who can afford to go to college. He is there because it is the natural place for him to be, not because the life of reason beckons, or because he wants to grow up to be a professor, or because curiosity is his master passion. His being there is important. His education is important. But whether he becomes a "scholar" or not is not important.

Second, speaking of the faculty, a "scholar" is not a "teacher"; a "professor" is not a "pedagogue." A scholar is a man with something on his mind and with the skill and determination to pursue it; a teacher is a cultivator of other minds. A university usually hires scholars and hopes that they will do as teachers.

Third, the administration is not the bureaucratic agent of alien claims upon the academic community. It is, on the whole, the conscientious guardian of the integrity of the institution, negotiating support while fending off distorting influence from the outside and confronting internal self-interest with the legitimate claims of the institution. It is, on the whole, probably too weak; and its "corruption," its misuse of the institution, is invariably less than that of the faculty and of the students.

The radical improvement of educational life within the university is not a narrow technical matter. It involves the reorganization and redirection of educational energies within an institution whose members and resources are already fully engaged in activity believed to be significant. No one is going to wipe the slate clean and start all over. Whether desirable or not, no quick, drastic, or massive change is likely. For to change education is to change the behavior of the faculty. Minor change, of course, is continually taking place. New courses are created, programs are renovated or reconstructed, lectures improve and deteriorate, requirements are changed; but the basic pattern is much the same.

EXPERIMENT AT BERKELEY

PART ONE

The American college must rediscover and renew its commitment to its fundamental purpose. It has a purpose, and that purpose is, for the sake of all of us, for society and for the individual, to develop our rational powers, to heighten sensitivity to and awareness of fundamental human problems, to cultivate and strengthen the habits and dispositions which make it possible for humanity to displace the varieties of warfare with the institutions, the practices, and the spirit of reasoning together. The college is not the blind or servile tool of transient arrangements, but it is not neutral as between reason and unreason, between freedom and frenzy, between civilization and chaos. It stands with Apollo, not with Dionysus.

The college must rediscover its purpose and must assert itself. It is not the marketplace which it has come, all too often, to resemble: professors crying their separate wares in their separate stalls, student customers wandering and loitering through the maze, consulting private shopping lists. We like the marketplace; it strikes us as an ideal situation—a social institution which caters to private desire. Let us have the market if we must, but let us not confuse it with the college. Free men are not produced in stores.

Nor is the college a professional school. It may prepare for, but it does not directly train for, the great professions. It has its own mission: to fit us for the life of active membership in the democratic community; to fit us to serve, in its broadest sense, our common political vocation.

A college consists of *faculty* and *students* appropriately related by and involved in a plan or *program of study*. This would seem to be an irreducible trinity, but there are heresies abroad in the land which, in one way or another, are anti-trinitarian.

The familiar "personalist" heresy runs something like this: it is all a matter of human relations, of communication—the teacher and student relating as persons, breaking through the artificial barriers of roles and authority and engaging in dialogue in small discussion groups, preferably unstructured. That gets rid of the program of study. If the faculty won't play, the attempt at transgenerational tolerance or understanding is abandoned and stress is placed on peer group interaction—"students educate each other." That gets rid of the faculty. In some versions the "others" disappear altogether and we are left with the solitary individual in search of himself.

There are, no doubt, other versions and other heresies, but I shall take it as obvious that the college has a faculty and that it has students (although there are some utopian visions. . .) . That there is always a program of study must be asserted with less confidence. Students always have work to do, but a miscellaneous collection of courses does not constitute a program. The deficiency, is most serious at the lower-division level, and it calls for drastic treatment.

The attempt to create a coherent first program brings to the test the entire range of educational resources and ideas. It imposes tasks upon the faculty which require it to re-examine its teaching theory and practice; it forces a reconsideration of the status and the needs of students; and it calls for a re-examination of basic curricular conceptions. That re-examination, if we undertake it, may revitalize our higher education.

I. The Teacher

The art of teaching, in its broadest sense, is the art of creating and maintaining an environment and a structure of activity conducive to the proper development of the mind. The teacher himself is an active feature of that environment and he applies energy and judgment in different ways at different points to stimulate growth and development. Teaching resembles gardening, except for the propensity to lecture to the roses.

The individual teacher tends to take the institutional environment as given—by the nature of things, by tradition, or by administrative decision tests the system for flexibility, accommodates himself with varying degrees of eccentricity to its limits, and settles for jurisdiction over his own courses as providing the arena within which he practices his art. *His* course, *his* subject, *his* students. Left largely to his own devices, the teacher comes to identify good teaching with "giving good courses." He masters a subject and develops a way of dealing with it. He lays out a course of study and sets out to be helpful—to sustain interest, to analyze and explain, to encourage and correct. He develops and comes to terms with his powers as a lecturer, works out a mode of individual consultation, and learns to accept with remarkable patience the shortcomings, the gratuitous indifference, and the occasional cruelty of students.

Undergraduate liberal arts teaching accommodates itself to the structure of the course and develops some distinctively course-related characteristics. It is necessary to mention the obvious because the course is so pervasive that we have come to regard the conditions of course teaching as the conditions of teaching in general.

The course forces teaching into small, relatively self-contained units. Horizontally, courses are generally unrelated and competitive. That is, the student is taking three or four or even five courses simultaneously. They are normally in different subjects, given by different professors, and, with rare exceptions, there is no attempt at horizontal integration. Thus, each professor knows that he has a valid claim to only a small fraction of a student's time and attention. The effect is that no teacher is in a position to be responsible for, or effectively concerned with, the student's total educational situation. The student presents himself to the teacher in fragments, and not even the advising system can put him together again.

What is worse is that the professor knows that even his fragment of the student's time must be competitively protected. If he does not make tangible, time-consuming demands the student diverts time to courses which do make such demands. It becomes almost impossible to set a reflective, contemplative, deliberate pace in a single course. The tendency is to over-assign work, with the expectation that it will probably not all be done. The cumulative effect on the student is brutal. To survive he must learn how to not do his work; he is forced into the adoption of the strategies of studentship; he learns to read too fast, to write and speak with mere plausibility. His educational life, through no fault of his own, becomes a series of artificial crises.

Horizontal competitiveness and fragmentation of student attention are limiting conditions of which every sensitive teacher is bitterly aware. But there is nothing he can do about it. He can develop a coherent course, but a collection of coherent courses may be simply an incoherent collection. For the student, to pursue one thread is to drop another. He seldom experiences the delight of sustained concentration. He lives the life of a distracted intellectual juggler.

The vertical aspect of the course structure mitigates, in principle, the separateness or independence of the individual course by providing sequences and treating some courses as prerequisite to others. The student, in this dimension, moves from the introductory through the intermediate to the advanced. While some sequences are obvious—as, for example, foreign language study—it is not always the case that the sequence is technically developmental. It may be a movement from a preliminary survey, historical or systematic, to courses with a narrower focus; and in such cases the preliminary course is not indispensable. The student may wish to go directly to the more specialized course, and the professor may be glad to admit someone who is interested in his subject and may waive the general introductory prerequisite.

Thus, while vertical sequence, integration, and development are features of the course structure, they are not as significant or pervasive as might appear. With some exceptions, courses come in clusters rather than in chains. The bearing of this on the planning function (or burden) of the faculty is significant. A chain takes more planning than a cluster. The internal structure of a particular course is more affected by its position in a chain or sequence of courses than by its location in a cluster. The former requires some faculty cooperation; the latter permits greater teaching autonomy. The faculty, like any group, finds cooperation difficult and prefers autonomy. Thus, in the absence of strong countervailing forces, a natural law of the universe finds expression in the curricular law, "chains give way to clusters."

The point is that such sequential organization as exists tends to be fairly loose, takes the course as its building block, and does not dominate its internal structure. The course is identified and located by name or subject and number. There are some college rules about courses and some departmental policies, but within those limiting conditions, the professor can shape his course as he thinks best. He practices the art of teaching within a quarter course which constitutes about 1/45th of the student's undergraduate education.

The teacher is thus stationed at a particular time and place in the educational process. Students come and go; he tends his station. It is inevitable that the rhetoric of discontent should seize upon the "cafeteria" and the "factory" as telling metaphors. It is also obvious that the criticism or defense of the quality of the courses offered is really beside the point. The difficulty is not with the quality of the particular course but with the course structure itself.

Even within these limitations there is a lot of good teaching going on. Professors normally put a great deal of thought and effort into their courses. Their devotion and diligence keep an essentially absurd system afloat. Their efforts may be appreciated, but they are seldom celebrated.

What usually comes to attention and acclaim as "great teaching" is a more spectacular sort of performance. "Performance" is the right word. The "great teacher" is, all too often, a great performer on stage. Articulate, witty, rhetorically versatile, he captures and holds his audience. He has ideas, and he makes the most of them. His course is a good show, and he usually plays to a full house. He is not necessarily eccentric, although there is a familiar type who is academically unconventional—the "professor as rebel." He attacks his colleagues, his guild, his discipline, his institution, his society. He is original about grades, examinations, schedules. His course is a charmingly defiant exercise in self-expression and self-indulgence. *He* has not been conquered by the system. But he confuses "students" with "audience."

It is a commonplace that the university does not sufficiently recognize and reward good undergraduate teaching. The university feels quite guilty about it and is always trying to make up for its neglect. But the instinct which keeps it from freely bestowing tenure and promotion for "good teaching" alone is, I think, quite canny. On the one hand, there is the generally invisible but adequate—even good—course teaching; on the other hand, there is the star performer. The former is not worth rewarding because course teaching itself is, as I have suggested, a generally fruitless form of teaching; the latter we are reluctant to reward—although we do reward it anyway—because something tells us, although we are afraid it may be jealousy, that there is something suspicious about it. It is as if we had some awards to bestow for excellence in swimming and found ourselves confronting candidates who on the one hand were managing to keep afloat in a well or who, on the other hand, seemed to be walking on water. Treading water and walking on it are peculiar kinds of swimming. Tending the courses that mark the stations of the student's cross and giving brilliant lectures are peculiar kinds of teaching. They are, I suspect, adequately rewarded.

We have gotten about as far as the course can take us. Energy spent in improving them produces only marginal gains and is energy misdirected. We have reached the point at which, if we are to improve college education significantly, we must create a real alternative to the course system itself and reduce the course to a peripheral feature of the educational structure. The only effective unit for educational planning is the program. And the Experimental Program has shown that it can be done even where it is most difficult—at the lower-division level.

A program of sufficient scope drastically alters the teaching situation, eliminates some problems entirely, and presents us with interesting new challenges.

First, the competitive horizontal pressures are removed. A single outside course can be accommodated without distraction (although more than a single course would probably destroy everything). Attention can be focused or concentrated, and decisions about simultaneous lines of activity can be made within the program on purely educational grounds. We can make possible exclusive attention to a single work for a sustained period. We can integrate or coordinate virtually the entire range of the student's academic activity—reading and writing, lecture and discussion. We can set our own pace and establish our own rhythm.

Vertically, continuity for a two-year period seems about right. While a single year is better than nothing, the second year brings to fruition and reinforces what the first year only begins. Two years is far more than merely twice as good as a single year. Such continuity provides ample opportunity to develop curricular themes and variations and to ensure variety and balance. It also makes possible a relaxed, confident, long-range approach to the development of particular skills and powers. We can, for example, think in terms of a sustained two-year program of writing. Development is discernible and can be fostered.

The program, unlike the course, is a workable educational unit. It presents us with the whole student for a significant period of time. It restores to the teacher a rather frightening share of responsibility for the student's education—a responsibility which seems to evaporate from the interstices of the course system. Educational decisions become necessary; more importantly, they become possible. The program recaptures for the teacher the possibility of giving a reasonable structure to the life of learning.

The shift from the course to the program has, however, a revolutionary effect on the teaching situation. A single professor can teach a course; he cannot teach a program. "What should I do with my students?" gives way to "What should we do with *ours*?" Unless structural reform entails the substitution of the latter question for the former, it will have only minor effects on the quality of education. We must move from individualistic to colleagial teaching. That is a drastic move, indeed; "revolutionary" is not an exaggeration.

We sometimes speak of a faculty as a "community of scholars," and the expression is, as often as not, used with irony. "Community" applied to scholars is like "pride" applied to lions or "school" applied to fish. But we do not even *say* "community of teachers." Scholars may collaborate and cooperate. But teaching, even after we make the necessary exceptions and qualifications, is normally regarded as a solo performance. The program necessitates the collaborative teaching which the individual course prevents or discourages. It involves professors in a genuinely common teaching enterprise. It gives the teacher real working colleagues.

Anyone familiar with the facts of academic life is more likely to shudder at this prospect than to welcome it. One's colleague is one's cross. The faculty meeting—college, departmental, or committee—is a familiar butt of academic literature. It is the abrasive ordeal from which one flees to the delicious, healing privacy of one's own course. There, the teacher cultivates his own field in peace. Publication subjects scholarship or research to the judgment of one's peers; the privacy of the classroom shields teaching from the critical scrutiny of colleagues.

Even academic freedom seems to be involved. Academic freedom, properly understood, is a doctrine which assures to the academic institution the power necessary for the performance of its function and freedom from improper external interference. It is a grant of autonomy to the institution not in order that it may do as it pleases, but in order that it may best do what it is supposed to do. The institution is empowered to exercise its own best judgment in fulfilling its responsibilities.

The academic institution has its own system of internal government. Some decisions are made collectively—by the school, or college, or department. And some matters, by a delegation of institutional authority, are left to the judgment and decision of the individual faculty member. He is, in some areas and to some degree, self-governing or autonomous. That autonomy is highly valued and gives to academic life much of its distinctive character. The professor in full cry is pretty much his own master.

But the claim to autonomy as a teacher does not stand on quite the same ground as the claim to autonomy as a scholar. A collection of scholarly experts is not a collection of expert teachers. The college professor is a professional scholar but only an amateur teacher. Autonomy in the classroom is not strongly buttressed by claims to expertness in "teaching." I am not proposing that we invade the classroom. I do suggest, however, that the claim to teaching autonomy is less firmly based than the claim to scholarly autonomy.

The course taught by a single professor is not sanctified by the law of nature; it is not a mandate of the charter of academic freedom; it is not triumphantly vindicated by its fruits. It is simply a customary, archaic mode of academic organization. It is supported by our habits, and it confirms us in our vices. It puts the professor, wrapt (rapt!) in his subject on the center of the stage, converts him into a verbose performer, and pawns this off as a paradigm of the life of reason.

The program gives us the teaching colleagues we so badly

need and imposes collective responsibility at the working level. Faculty egos check each other, with the inevitable result that the student, not the performer, moves into the center of the picture. The teacher finds himslf worrying less about what to say next than about what the students should be doing next. Genuine teaching problems move onto the faculty agenda, and teaching practice, under the stimulus of example, discussion, and criticism, improves steadily. The experience is both exhausting and exhilarating. It can shake the teacher rather strongly, but it can only improve him.

Our interim reports express concern about staffing difficulty as affecting the future of the Experimental Program. It is, I think, the only real problem we have, and it has two aspects. First, can enough regular members of the existing institution be convinced of the value of the enterprise and be freed from other claims upon their time and energy? And second, can we surmount the internal difficulties which faculty cooperation in a common teaching program present? In its short three-year history, the Experimental Program has been shaken by both sets of difficulties. The program has survived and is, at the moment, thriving. But the problem remains.

Some aspects of the situation are revealed by a brief account of our staffing history. While the program was in the process of being approved five regular members of the Berkeley faculty had agreed to try the experiment. They all had good reputations as teachers. They did not, of course, come together spontaneously. I invited each one to join in developing and implementing the tentatively defined project. Three were able to commit themselves for the full two-year period; the other two, for a single year. Together, we selected five teaching assistants for a one-year trial period. By the end of the first year, we had decided to proceed without teaching assistants. To replace the two members with one-year commitments and the teaching assistants, we added three faculty members. Two were from Berkeley and the third was a visiting professor brought in for a year specifically for the program.

Toward the end of the second year, it was decided to continue the program for another two-year cycle. My efforts to recruit a staff from among the regular Berkeley faculty failed completely. Rather than abandon the program, I was authorized to gather a well-qualified "visiting" staff for a two-year period. I called on friends in other universities and they came to the rescue. This group, by good fortune, will remain intact for the two-year period. The implications seem overwhelming, but all is not yet lost. I will have more to say about this situation below.

The problems of internal cooperation are far more interesting. The first year was traumatic, marked by deep and trying conflict; the second year was a year of armed truce; and the third year was an unforgettable year of triumphant cooperative teaching. We have learned something about the ground rules.

A program must be based on and dominated by a single, fairly simple, curricular conception. That conception must have, so to speak, constitutional status, and it must remain beyond challenge for the duration of a cycle. Fundamental questions must be faced in the process of conception and the answers, however tentative, must be embodied in the constitution of the program. Fundamental changes may be warranted by experience, but they cannot be made in mid-stream except—if there is an exception at all—by the unanimous and genuinely uncoerced consent of the staff.

The constitutional conception must be the basis upon which the faculty is gathered or recruited. Whether it is framed by one person or by a group, no one should be invited or allowed to teach in the program unless he commits himself to its basic terms.

The point is not to make disagreement impossible; it is rather to make disagreement possible and fruitful. We can only disagree within the program if we agree about it. Constitutional disagreement while a program is in process threatens to destroy it; "legislative" disagreement (if we may use that contrast) can enrich it. While many decisions can be left open to be made by the faculty as it proceeds, the constitutional structure must be decided from the start.

The importance of constitutional clarity and commitment cannot, I think, be too strongly insisted upon. The faculty member is an individualist. He not only has ideas, he is used to being able to act on them. In a common program he cannot do everything his own way, but his tendency will be to attempt to re-create the conditions within which he is habitually successful and at ease. Differences in teaching style and practice are deep-seated, and they are usually supported, if questioned, by a theory of education. In a teacher of any experience—especially a successful teacher—to challenge them is to challenge *him*. Many views of teaching are incompatible with each other. In a system of individual courses that does not matter; but some differences make teaching together impossible. Constitutional clarity can prevent some disasters.

Even so, we can count on misunderstandings which will raise fundamental questions and will pose some threats to the program. One danger is that the faculty will split into factions on the nature of the program. And that kind of disagreement, on top of the normal range of problems, is almost too much to live with. If decision is forced "politically" the losers can become disaffected and withdraw spiritually from the common effort. If, to avoid that, we try to compromise, the result is, like any educational compromise, a mess which pleases no one, and which makes one long for his private course where at least *someone's* conception of what is best can be controlling. Factionalism and compromise are the banes of the common program, and prior constitutional clarity and agreement are the necessary inoculation.

The "constitution," overbearing as it may seem in this account, really contains little except what is necessary to preserve the common enterprise and encourage fruitful interaction: (1) a central curricular conception, about which I shall say more later, and, as a corollary, the understanding that all students are to study the same thing at the same time. That is, no special reading list for "one's own" students. If in the judgment of a faculty member something should be added (or omitted) he must raise the matter for common consideration and decision; (2) a single, common lecture program in which all participate and which all attend. This is an especially valuable unifying force. (3) A single, common schedule of seminars, conferences, and writing.

These principles protect the common program against the tendency to become fragmented internally, force the faculty to develop and apply collective judgment to common educational problems, and provide sufficient stability to encourage freshness and flexibility.

Each faculty group will, of course, develop its own institutions of discussion, deliberation, and decision. It was not until the third year of the Experimental Program that we developed a really successful pattern. Its elements include:

(1) Prior summer support so that the faculty can prepare itself for the program. This permits some intensive planning of the curricular and pedagogic pattern and time for preparatory reading and study.

(2) During the teaching year, provision for regular faculty

meetings. A meeting over coffee for a half-hour prior to the lecture twice a week is sufficient to take care of most minor matters. But the significant institution is the faculty "seminar." Once each week, through the entire academic year, the faculty met for dinner and discussion. Mostly, we discussed the program reading, argued about the ideas involved, and considered their educational significance. In spite of the heat which was sometimes generated, these meetings—which normally lasted about four hours—were delightful and exciting. The seminar shaped and supported the lecture program, brought out the issues, and made individual experience and insight the common property of the program. It is not too much to say that, in fact, the seminar *made* the program. In retrospect, much of the internal difficulty during the first two years seems due to the fact that we had not yet developed the regular evening faculty seminar.

If a program faculty develops the proper *esprit de corps* it will, I believe, seldom find itself voting about anything. It is a small group and attitudes quickly become known. It is genuinely colleagial and, given the constitutional commitment, questions of formal democracy or equality seem quite irrelevant. Consensus usually emerges from full and free discussion, and when it does not and some decision is necessary it is probably better to let someone express the decision of the group than to count heads. If *that* becomes an important question itself, the faculty is in trouble, and counting heads—although it can be done—won't help much. Voting, in an educational program, is only for matters which are not worth discussion.

The rewards of involvement in a successfully functioning group are very great. It is an unforgettable experience. It is also an experience of unusual intellectual and psychological intimacy which can, if things do not go well, be very trying. Personal sensitivity, pride, vanity, insecurity are always with us, and friendship is an indispensable balm. Friendship is, in fact, an important recruiting principle and should be recognized as a legitimate one.

This sketch of the internal situation may suggest some of the reasons for difficulty in recruiting faculty members to teach in programs. It sounds a little like trying to convert the prosperous small businessman to socialism. Moreover, the Experimental Program, in tackling the problem where college education is at its worst, in the lower division, faces special difficulties.

Let me refer again to what I have called the "three program" structure of the university. This consists of the graduate program, the upper-division major program, and the largely non-existent lower division or first program.

To some extent the graduate or third program already embodies principles upon which the Experimental Program is based. It is not generally course-dominated and it involves vertical continuity over a sustained period of time with only minimal horizontal distraction. It is subject to and even requires cooperative staff planning and direction.

The major, or second program, places at the disposal of the department roughly half of the student's academic time over a two-year period. The educational potentialities of this situation are in most cases unrealized because departments usually define the major program in terms of sequences or clusters of individual courses. But there is very little standing in the way of a department's deciding to organize its major program differently—to assign a tutorial staff to an appropriate number of students for a two-year period and to commission that staff to work out a two-year program of common reading, writing, and discussion. This is well within departmental discretion and would raise very few, if any, legislative, staffing, or budgetary problems.

The second and third programs have two very significant advantages over the first program from the point of view of program development. First, each is based upon or rooted in an established academic subject, field, or discipline, centered in an academic department. This simplifies the curricular problem considerably. And second, the department provides us with a continuing corps of disciplinary experts who expect to, are prepared to, and are even eager to teach their "subjects."

The special problems of the first program are revealed by contrast. Its curriculum does not coincide with an academic subject or fall within a department's discipline. And, since the college faculty is departmentally organized and recruited, there is no easily available or continuing first-program staff.

To involve a member of a department in a first program requires that he be able, for a time, to free himself from his normal departmental responsibilities and also that he be willing, for a time, to work outside the area of his specialization. These are formidable obstacles.

But the lower division is an educational wasteland. We cannot abandon there whatever is left of the possibility of liberal education. The first-program conception can save it, and we cannot accept present obstacles as permanent barriers. There are, I believe, two complementary possibilities which, if pursued, might make at least a dent in the problem.

First, we must devote more attention to, and learn to deliberately reap the benefits of, the distinctive phases of the normal academic career. That a professor moves through intellectual phases is a fact not a disgrace. But it is sometimes supposed that he should race continuously and triumphantly on the straight and narrow path on which he starts and that to waver or to leave that path is to begin to decay and die. That is not quite the correct description of the civilization of a barbarian or of the development of a mind. The mind, too, has its seasons, and the periodic breaking in of wisdom redirects and alters the mode in which we pursue knowledge. An analytic, technical mood gives way, for a time, to a reflective or synthesizing mood. There are times of assessment and reorientation as well as times of confident exploration.

The professor is not, therefore, at all times or at all stages fit for the same kind of teaching activity. There is a time for graduate students and there is a time for freshmen—graduate students when he is developing knowledge, freshmen when he is seeking wisdom.

The task of educational administration is to provide opportunities for teaching which correspond with the phases of the teacher's career and to facilitate and encourage flexible and timely involvement with first-, second-, and third-program teaching.

Fortunately, the phase of the academic career during which the institutional and personal pressures operate most strongly against first-program involvement is also the phase during which the professor is least fit for first-program teaching. There is a good deal of misplaced regret over the fact that junior members of the faculty, the assistant professoriate, are under heavy pressures of research and publication. "Publish or perish" is not entirely a myth, but we often overlook the fact that it does not express merely an external institutional demand. The decisive pressures are internal. The candidate for academic life is a professional intellectual in his novitiate. He is interested in knowledge, attracted by ideas, anxious to solve problems. He *wants* to make a significant contribution in his chosen field. He is eager, driving, ambitious, enthusiastic. It is likely to be a decade before he emerges from his first great "technical" phase. During that initial phase he is best suited for graduate or upper-division teaching. He is likely to be more specialized than he will be later and should probably be encouraged to mine his particular vein to its limit before he is diverted by teaching demands that require a different frame of mind. Junior teaching energy tends to be most professional and, in character, furthest removed from first-program teaching. It is fresh and enthusiastic; but it is also likely to be subject-centered, self-centered, and missionary.

So we should not waste too much time and energy bemoaning, or fighting, the difficulties of freeing the junior faculty for first-program teaching. We should look to the tenure ranks in terms of both suitability and availability. Readiness for ventures into first-program teaching should be seen as marking the end of academic adolescence.

It must be acknowledged, however, that there are many members of faculties who are really never fit for first-program teaching. They are merely scholars, specialists, technicians without mitigating philosophic or reflective resources. They have an honored place in the university. They may be quite productive in the current mode of their discipline, and they play a large part in the training of graduate students. But they have one-track minds, and if derailed they simply come to a stop. Whether he is still a rampant young lion or is subsiding into "old Blank who is still doing research in X," he is not much interested in teaching callow freshmen who aren't "motivated." He believes in scholarship and in his discipline (as he knows it, or knew it), scorns the dilettante, and wouldn't be caught dead outside his special field. He is useful where he is, and is best left undisturbed. He does not understand the first program and is opposed to it by instinct. The university is full of such citizens who will never be suitable or "ready" for the first program.

And second, we must, to take advantage of such faculty readiness as there may be, provide a first program structure-in-being with which a willing faculty member can easily associate himself.

The only feasible solution is, I believe, to establish, in one way or another, a regular first-program core-staff. To develop a separate lower-division or first-program faculty would, apart from other objections, defeat the purpose of encouraging the regular faculty to move through the whole range of teaching situations. But to have no permanent staff at all to provide experience, continuity, and stability would mean that we would have few, if any, first programs at all.

This conclusion has been reached with great reluctance. But faith in the continuous spontaneous generation of programs is now dead. The obstacle course is too difficult.

A permanent core-staff would have responsibility for developing and modifying program constitutions, for recruiting faculty to join in the program for a period of one or two years, and for providing leadership for the teaching staff. If we consider a normal program as involving six faculty and 150 students, we should plan on a core-staff of two or three for each faculty group of six. Two is certainly a minimum.

It should be said that this account of the staffing difficulties reflects the special bias and condition of a university with a dominant graduate school and upper-division concern. The regular four-year college has easier solutions at hand, and the lower-division junior or community college can shift to a program basis quite easily, if it can free itself from the tyranny of transfer requirements.

It is clear, I think, that the problem of establishing the first program is quite extrinsic to its educational merit. If the program were only as good as, or slightly better than, the present pattern of lower-division education, it would not be worth bothering with. It is not just a little better. It is infinitely better.

The difficulty is due entirely to the established teaching habits of the contemporary professoriate and to the institutional structure which reflects and reinforces those habits. Those habits—as *teaching* habits—are appalling; they need reformation. But the case is one in which the physician must heal himself. No one else can really do it. The gradual replacement of the individual course by the common program is probably the only real therapeutic device on the scene.

But all this sounds unnecessarily and misleadingly grim. The life of the faculty in the program is deeply exciting, satisfying, and refreshing. What, after all, does he do? It is a full-time commitment, so, for a year or two, he puts other things aside. He reads and studies, with other faculty members and with students, a coherent and varied sequence of great, readable books dealing with the great human questions. He joins in a lively faculty seminar. He discusses what we read with students. He reads and confers with students about their papers. He gives occasional informal lectures. He is an active member of a genuine working community, involved with people and with ideas. He is still a teacher, but he sees, in a different context, what the art of teaching really is. Life in the program is, without question, a great and unique experience.

II. The Student

Students en masse are apparently a disturbing spectacle. Beards and mini-skirts, mysterious potions and simple musical instruments, evoke ancestral memories of nymphs and satyrs. In our puritan nightmare they have emerged from the wooded fringes and swarm unheeding and shameless in the public streets, the parks, and the campus—dazed or frenzied litterers. Or, in the other nightmare, the sullen cast of *Lear*—Gonerils, Edmunds, Regans—monsters of ingratitude, are turning heedless and destructive energy against the aging nurturer.

The college, when it is not blamed for causing all this, is at least expected to cure it. And the danger to the college, as it comes in crisis to the center of public attention, is that its own internal efforts to understand and to improve itself will be impeded by the overwhelming emphasis on visible disorder. Of course disorder is a serious problem. But it may be the symptom of deeper problems and stirrings, and we must aim at more than a premature subsiding of symptoms.

The college is the point at which three parties meet and make demands of each other. These parties are, in fact, deeply interdependent, and the college is, in principle, a point of cooperative integration. If it has come to resemble a battlefield it is because each party comes with two sets of banners—one set authentic, the other a subtle caricature which, when raised, seems authentic enough, but by insensible degree breeds chaos.

First, society *is* a party to the college and to meet society's legitimate demands is not a betrayal. It asks the college to prepare successive generations to carry on and develop the life of the culture, to provide for both continuity and change, for appreciation and criticism, for transmission and creation. That is the authentic banner, and who cannot rally to it? But the caricature is different. It says "accept," "conform," and "who pays the piper?" and it gets the response it merits.

The second party is the faculty, the keeper of the college. Its task is complicated, and its corruptions are subtle. I shall not linger here but will put the matter crudely. Its authentic banner says "cultivate wisdom"; its seductive caricature says "pursue knowledge." (Or perhaps "be reasonable," and "be inquisitive.") And the difference in emphasis eventually converts a college of intelligent teachers into a collection of mere scholars.

Finally, the student. He is a party to the college. He is there, and importantly there, although transitory. He is there because we care about him, because he needs special treatment, and because the life he may live is not altogether his own.

When all is right with the world, the student, who is, after all, a student, sees the college as a school and respects its character as a place of tutelage. When times are out of joint, he may see it simply as his place, his scene, his city and, in a premature rejection of tutelage, raise the counterfeit banner of self-determination, autonomy, democracy, play generational house, or sally forth to claim and change the corrupt old world. Moses, descending from the heights, faces the crisis of the golden calf—the schism between those who think that the journey toward freedom still lies ahead and those who think they have arrived. School, he declares, is not over.

It is not necessary to imagine what it would be like if everything went wrong and the hosts were marshalled under the counterfeit banners. It has happened, and the tumult is all too familiar and, by now, boring. Outraged society pounds the table and growls for order and discipline; the faculty is busy doing research; and the students are beating their chests and chasing their tails. The American college of the '60's.

Serious discussion of education in this situation is almost impossible. The noise level is too high, and we are soon shouting at each other. How can we discuss and maintain the delicate relations between the society and the college in an atmosphere marked by fear and suspicion on one side and defiant dependence on the other? How can the faculty clarify its responsibilities to society and to its students when, enthralled by the pursuit of knowledge as an end in itself, it sees their claims as secondary and distracting importunities? How can we expect students, in this atmosphere of competitive self-assertion, to lend themselves to purposes other than their own, to not see themselves as a neglected interest group whose hopes depend on the assertion of student power? Initiation into what? Tutelage for what?

Reasoning together is displaced by negotiation, and the campus of the future, we are told, will rediscover "community" only by accepting a pressure group view of itself and by admitting, in the name of freedom and democracy, the once silent and oppressed majority to the corridors and seats of governance. But the view of the college as a political democracy is nonsense. It may be, at this time, unconquerable nonsense, but it is nonsense none the less. Of course, a college is really not "undemocratic" either. The concept is simply inapplicable, and anyone who knows what a college is understands the point. "Democracy" applied to a college makes about as much sense as "democracy" applied to a rainbow or to a baseball game.

The effect of the prevalence of this nonsense is that education in the college is now under the pressure of misguided student demands which, even when educationally motivated, are so imbued with a consumer-oriented pressure group quasi-democratic ideology as to place only another set of obstacles in the path of real educational reform.

These demands are, in large measure, going to be granted. Administrations, accustomed to dealing with pressures, are prepared, or soon will be, to deal with one pressure group more. They have, quite properly, considerable concern about students, and they know better than the faculties that the students have valid complaints about education. Long experience has taught them that the organized faculty is too strong to be moved educationally by administrative effort. Student-faculty "encounter" may at least bring some countervailing power to the table and produce more change than can be produced by the usual application of administrative energy to faculty inertia.

The faculty member, on the other hand, is quite prepared to make concessions which do not require him to change his way of life, which do not restrict his authority over his own course or class. There is a whole set of currently fashionable student demands which have that virtue—more student control over "student affairs," more freedom from formal requirements, credit for student-initiated courses; and supporting those demands has some attractions. "After all, it is only simple justice. Here am I, doing what I want. Why shouldn't the student do what he wants? Who am I to impose my values on him? He has watched television all his life, and he's an adult now. What he does on his own time is his own business. Why ask him to study what he's not interested in? Who likes a captive audience in a required course? Why not let him initiate courses if he can find some faculty member who feels like taking it on? Why not give him credit for going to Mississippi? He might learn something. If we grant all this, maybe things will calm down. And if I vote "Yes," I can be a liberal educational reformer." Seldom in the history of education has reform required so little of so many.

The argument is almost irresistable, and the student, I am afraid, is doomed to get what he wants. Or thinks he wants. Instead of curing the disease, it will simply move us into its final stages.

I am reluctant to waste much time trying to meet the argument for the further extension of the principle of laissez-faire in the college. The principle itself is disastrously inappropriate for education and its further extension is merely a depressing exercise in futility. To dress it in the rhetoric of freedom, democracy, and community is to indulge in sick parody approaching blasphemy.

The college is still a place of schooling. To affirm this is not necessarily to deny the adulthood of the student but rather to assert its irrelevance. Students come to us in various stages of development—physical, emotional, intellectual. In some respects they are quite mature, although American culture does not notably value or encourage the dubious blessing of early maturation. Very little follows educationally from the explicit assertion of adulthood, although, since adolescents are so touchy about it, it is tactless to deny it. Facing the facts about time, with equanimity, is hard even for adults who have had more time to get used to them.

Perhaps the only significant point about maturity is its bearing upon educational motivation. With infants and children we exploit "interest"; with adults "purpose" becomes dominant, and we hear less of "but I'm not interested in . . ." as a reason for lack of educational engagement. The adult has learned that interest develops with and sustains fruitful activity; it does not necessarily initiate or guide it. The "not interested" whine is the dirge of the undeveloped mind, and the elective system panders without nourishing. As a solution to educational hunger it is candy for children. To treat students as adults is to not worry so much about their views about what they are interested in.

If we consider, beyond this, the wisdom of placing upon the student, adult or not, the burden of constructing the mosaic of his own education out of the mass of discrete courses in the catalogue, the answer is obvious. It is not lack of intelligence or lack of maturity, but lack of experience and knowledge which is decisive. The college has no right to evade its responsibility for educational planning by the specious device of treating the student as an adult who should plan his own education.

As for student-initiated courses, they are just courses, probably all right as courses go, probably inferior to faculty-initiated courses. Not much harm, not much gain; a pointless diversionary move which allows some youthful energy to spend itself in premature educational entrepreneurship. It only strengthens the course system and does not improve education. It is not worth fighting for, or against.

So much for shadow boxing with folly under the counterfeit banners.

The crux is freedom. Liberal education aims at the free mind. Every aspect and device of the Experimental Program is intended to serve that end. If we could force men to be free, we would; as it is, we can only try to help them. Once we understand what freedom of the mind is, the paradoxical quality of that statement disappears. Minds are not made free by being left alone. Nor are students.

We are told that there are two concepts of freedom; one good and one bad, one simple, one complex, one safe, one dangerous. The nice freedom is, of course, the absence of coercion or external constraint. Chains and bars limit our freedom; laws, threats, and sanctions also constrain us. They limit our freedom by preventing us from doing as we wish. The fewer the barriers the greater the freedom. This is the simple and safe view. Even assuming that it is clear, it presents us with several small flaws. First, the mere removal of external barriers does not touch the disparity between the weak and the strong. How valuable is the absence of external restraint in the absence, as well, of positive power or capacity? And second, suppose one acts, in the absence of external restraint, in a way in which is harmful to oneself. In that case, freedom turns out to be bad for us.

Defenders of this conception of freedom may wish to meet the first point by embracing "equality" as a supplementary good or perhaps "equality of opportunity and the devil take the hindmost." As for the second point, you can't have everything! Freedom is good, but it includes the possibility of doing the wrong thing. Better to suffer and learn caution than to limit freedom; or if not, limit it a bit.

It turns out, apparently, that, on this view, freedom is not a "good" for the weak and foolish; he cannot do much and he is likely to do the wrong thing. It *is* a "good" for the strong and wise, for the "able."

It should not surprise us, therefore, that a second concept of freedom arises—one that seeks to define freedom so as to preserve its character as an unmitigated "good thing." It seizes on precisely these qualities which make the absence of external restraint a good thing—strength and wisdom—and defines the free man as one who has the power to achieve what is indeed good. This, of course, is the "positive" or dangerous view of freedom.

It is dangerous because, if government is to promote freedom, it may no longer be the case that that government is best which does the least; it must do something to develop the powers and the wisdom of its citizens; it must see to it that minds are cultivated; it must, in the almost unimaginable extreme case, create and maintain a system of public schools. It is a license to meddle.

Moreover, the "freedom" which once seemed so easy—laissez-faire, laissez-aller—now becomes something difficult, an achievement. It is not the sort of thing which someone can simply be given "now" by an act of Congress. To turn children loose is not to make them free. One is free to swim only if he knows how.

It is, of course, only freedom in this positive sense which is relevant to education. And that is not because educators are professional meddlers who cannot bear to leave people alone and who, therefore, prefer the "positive," the "welfare" or the "authoritarian" state to its less intrusive alternative. It is rather because the mind is not the sort of thing, or entity, or process, to which the notions of physical constraint (or barriers) apply. The mind is not something which can be held or pushed, except in a metaphoric sense. And the metaphor can easily mislead us. We can think of a body as moving freely when unobstructed and, in a materialist tradition, can describe a man as free when, unhindered, he can do what he wants or go where he wants to. We sometimes try to apply this notion to the mind and speak of the "freedom to believe." But it does not parse. Can we believe as we please? Only if we are insane. A healthy mind, a functioning mind, a free mind, is not a mind which believes as it pleases.

Thus, in thinking about the mind, or of the person, we can easily fall into a confusion of categories and systematically misuse the language of objects. About "freedom" the sin is habitual. For the mind to be free is for it to be able, to have the power, to do what it should do. That is the freedom with which education is concerned. For the student who seeks freedom, the implications are drastic. He must submit himself to the imperatives of the quest for genuine power. He must incorporate in himself the power of the culture of which he is the creature.

Satan's great flaw, in *Paradise Lost*, is his inability to enjoy the given. "Better to reign in Hell than serve in Heaven" is not the cry of a lover of freedom but of one who would reign at all costs and who does not understand what "serving in heaven" means. He is mixed up about freedom, power, and goodness, and the Pandemonium he creates is a dark parody of the order he rejects. He is enamoured only of his own creation and cannot accept the good when it comes as a gift. He is surly about gifts. His missing virtue is docility.

Docility, acquiescence, deference—these appear to our present mood as weakness if not vices, as pre-democratic attitudes, close kin to humility and respectfulness, conservative tools of exploitation and suppression. But they are in some circumstances really virtues, and their current disrepute is part of our problem.

Let me say at once that I consider docility to be a necessary element in the character of the healthy student. Docility is not merely a matter of obedience, although intelligent obedience is also necessary. It is a complex set of attitudes toward the world and the immediate context which is a condition of growth toward freedom. This has been expressed canonically in the promise that only the docile shall inherit the earth, that unruliness is self-defeating.

Docility is destroyed by fear or anxiety. It is a kind of spiritual relaxedness, a looseness, which comes from faith, hope, love, trust, confidence—from the sense that something good is going on and that one wants to, and can, join in. To *join in* what is going on, to be led in, inducted, initiated; not to destroy by breaking in and breaking up. Anyone who has watched an instructor teach skiing or tennis or swimming will find this very familiar. "Relax, relax. Don't fight it, use it. Try it this way and you'll see. Don't be afraid to . . . don't worry about . . . don't tighten up." What the pupil learns, if he learns at all, is that the world does most of the work, and that his job is to learn how to cooperate with it and to accommodate himself to its requirements if he wishes it to support his purposes. This piety of the body is the germ or paradigm of the more complex piety of the mind or spirit. "Docility" is, perhaps, a non-denominational or secular term for "piety."

Not fear, then, but a positive set of attitudes. Affirmation and enjoyment of what is good; acceptance, with shameless gratitude, of gifts, of goods we have not created but which are there for us; appreciation of the continuity and fellowship of human achievement; respect for the craft and its masters; the faith and trust of apprenticeship. These are the facets of docility.

Without docility we learn, if we learn at all, the hard way. If we do not let the world teach us, it teaches us a lesson. So it is, in tragedy, that the indocile—Creon, Oedipus, Lear—learn only through bitter suffering. Socrates suggested a better way.

Student indocility is a serious problem, but it is a sickness not a crime, and it cannot be cured by a lecture. If we wish to blame someone let us, at least, not blame the victims, but look to the social institutions and their trustees who have nourished disillusion, rejection, and distrust, and who generate alienation in absurdity instead of membership in community. The immediate question is whether the college can cope with indocility and even cure it, or whether its own structure and operation make it worse. The short answer, I believe, is that the standard lower-division structure makes it worse, but that the pattern established by the Experimental Program, while it cannot cope with everyone and everything, is fundamentally helpful.

The student who enters the program does so by his own decision. It is very much a decision taken in the dark, since he has no experience either of the program or its alternatives. But it is his own decision about his education and, if he remains in the program, it is the last administrative decision about education he is called upon to make for several years. Whether he realizes it or not he has, through an accidental combination of circumstances, committed himself to something by an act of faith.

The student finds himself in a program which is overwhelming in its givenness. Its curriculum is set and completely required, and he is not consulted about it. When he is curious or anxious about its general structure, he is given a correct general answer and told, also correctly, that he won't really understand the answer until he has been through the program.

We advise him to relax, to take things as they come, to try to enjoy the present, and that he will soon be catching the drift.

The structure of work, although it leaves much to the student, is also fixed and given and presents the student with a reasonable but inexorable schedule of writing, conference, discussion, and lecture. It is, for him, a novel pattern, and he is expected to adjust to it. It may take some time, but we do not waive the demands.

Early responses are, of course, quite varied, but we are now familiar with some significant symptoms and can even risk generalization. The "healthy" response seems to have two elements: first, the student is moved by what we are reading and is enjoying it, and second, he is discouraged by his inability to work as hard as he thinks he should be working and by the realization that his work, chiefly his writing, isn't very good. Both responses are encouraging signs. They reveal that he is accepting the task, not fighting it, and that he is open, perceptive, and even objective. We encourage the enjoyment, try to cheer him up about his performance, and settle down to constructive work.

The first symptom of trouble, on the other hand, is lack of enjoyment. It is not simply a matter of taste. If we are all reading and talking about Homer, for example, not to be enjoying it means that something is wrong. It may mean—and usually does—that the student is not reading or is not trying to read. Why not? At this point we begin to sense, in one form or another, the drive for autonomy, the existence or emergence of private plans, and even a strategy of self-defense. Why are we reading this instead of something else, why this kind of paper assignment, why so slow or so fast, can I do something else instead? General dissatisfaction with what is given. It should be stressed that this mood is more likely than not to be the accompaniment of not doing the work or at least not doing it very well, and also that the student may have a higher opinion of his written work than is warranted. That is, he is not happy with, engaged with, or enjoying the program, and he appears to be fairly satisfied with and defensive about the work he does. He is like a student who for some reason signs up for a tennis class, doesn't seem to enjoy the game, doesn't practice much, always thinks the teacher is doing the wrong thing, and is impervious to the teacher's criticism and judgment of his strokes.

This is the indocility problem, and it is not easy to deal with. We resist as long as possible the temptation to say simply, "If you don't like it here why don't you go somewhere else?" In any case, the answer is likely to be, "I don't like it there, either." The student is encased in armor which hinders his movement and growth, and our task is to free him if we can, and if he stands still long enough. But he is not always ready to get rid of his armor. It is home-made, fairly comfortable, and still useful for combat. His reasons for acquiring it are still operative and he distrusts the invitation to take it off. The world that lies before him seems rotten and hostile, the establishment is powerful and corrupt, and the college is its tool. He cannot relax.

The stultifying self-protective capacity of the indocile student is formidable. We try to create an environment in which trust is reasonable, and we practice patience. But in some cases nothing seems to work and the student never really gets involved, although this is not always marked by formal separation from the program. He may, as a rebel, move into the shrill culture of "activism" and learn its thin lessons. He may go completely, if temporarily, out of reach in the faubourgs of contemporary bohemia and learn the lessons of its illusions. Or he may find less dramatic ways of getting lost. We regret the foolish choices we cannot prevent.

The program is a better school, but it can be fought, resisted, or rejected by those who do not understand, or who lack the power to fulfill, the commitment of enrollment. "Commitment" is worth lingering over. There *is* a moral dimension to the problem. The program is a voluntary undertaking and there are reciprocal obligations. There are "oughts" for the faculty and "oughts" for the student which go far beyond mere academic criminal law. What is required is a good-faith effort. And there can be failure at three levels: misconception or failure to understand what an undertaking is, or that this is one; bad faith; and failure of effort. The last is merely a matter of weakness. We expect it and attend to it. The others pose deeper problems of morality.

I do not intend to pursue here the discussion of student academic morality, although it is underdiscussed. The theme is freedom and the free mind. To be free, I have argued, is to be able to do what one should. Lack of understanding, ill-will, and bad habits (or incapacity to work)—this is the simple profile of the unfree man. Freed from external restraint only his incapacity postpones disaster. In the incubator of the program we cherish docility. It is not all of virtue, nor its final form, but it is the embryonic precursor of freedom.

I turn now to an explanation of how the process of involvement in the program supports the student's growth in power or freedom.

Interest

The first problem is that of liberating the student from thralldom to his so-called interests. He may arrive under the impression that he knows what he is interested in and also that he knows that he is not interested in certain things. He may believe that he does well only in doing what he is interested in and he is inclined to want, naturally, to pursue his interests further. The student who "doesn't know what he is interested in" tends to be worried about his condition, is discouraged about his apathy, and is anxious to get interested in something, to "find himself."

Perhaps the worst thing that can happen to the student at the start of college life is that his interest-condition should be allowed to determine the shape of his education. The student arrives at college a creature of circumstance struggling to take charge of himself—of this time and that place, of home, town, school, friends, games, trials, triumphs, and errors. Interested in law, or medicine, or science, or literature? Why? A parent, a relative, a local hero, a television program? Did a high school teacher praise his verse? Was math easy? Did he fall in love with his motorcycle or have an underprivileged friend? Did girls like him? Was he too fat to run? Did he work for his allowance? Was his mother nervous? We should help spring him, if we can, from the trap of accident.

An interest, unlike a headache, is not an item of immediate indubitable awareness; it is not revealed by a simple act of introspection. Interests come in layers, they change and develop, they even come disguised. Knowledge of ourselves is a difficult achievement, and the deeper pattern of our interests may escape our scrutiny.

At what point and to what degree a student's conception of what he is interested in should be allowed to shape and direct his education is a difficult question. But it is, I am sure, a disastrous mistake to let it dominate or seriously influence the lower-division years. It will, at that stage confine and limit him.

The alternative, of course, is not to hurl our own discrete and varied interests at him, but rather to construct a required program which involves what he should be interested in. That is not as difficult or as ludicrous as it may sound. It is another way of saying that the curriculum should be about what is centrally important and that it should be deep and difficult. "Important" for the liberal-arts lower division in America today means "moral," "social," "political"; it means freedom and authority, the individual and society, conscience and law, acceptance and rebellion. That is what the student ought to be interested in and that is what he will find that he is interested in, although it may surprise him. "Deep" means that the curriculum must push beyond the current cliché and surface of the problem to its fundamental terms. "Difficult" means that it should be intelligible but inexhaustible.

In such a program the "interest" question gradually subsides or is displaced by the discovery that enjoyment is more crucial and is more likely to evoke interest than to be produced by it. The student grows less temperamental about his work, less finicky, more confidently omnivorous. His latent self gets some nourishment. Involvement in the program, given and required as it is, helps in removing the "interest" barrier from the path of development.

Habit, Power, Self-discipline

With rare exception the intellectual habits of the student who arrives at college are those of a defensive scrambler. His experience is primarily of crisis response to varied, fragmentary, unrelated demands. He has risen to these demands and crises or he wouldn't be where he is, but the experience has left its mark on him. He can marshall façades to meet tests. But his reading and writing habits show the effects. The crisis must be abated and the habits it generates must be displaced by others. Examination is a disciplinary device, but it is not the only one and is not in the long run a good one.

Unfortunately, the usual course pattern in the lower division continues the crisis pattern of the high school and even increases its pressure. Successful adjustment by the student only confirms him in bad habits. He may learn quite a lot, but he does not significantly gain in effective mastery of his intellectual energies. The senior, all too often, is simply a tired freshman who has been through the mill.

The Experimental Program breaks away from the usual pattern and provides a different environment for a sufficiently long time—two years—so that the student can gain, or regain, some effective autonomy on the basis of reasonable habit. We try, as far as possible, to avoid crisis, haste, and pressure. We have eliminated all examinations and tests; assignments are quantitatively light; grades are effectively out of the picture. The stage is set for a long, unharried pull.

The program is a set of clear and unavoidable demands presented at a steady pace—a regular schedule of reading, of discussion, of writing, which must be done on time. Constant timeliness, however, is our aim, not the mere meeting of deadline, although the deadline has its place. We really have no make-up devices. Our interdependence in a common program requires that we discipline ourselves to the common pace, that we keep current.

Old habits persist, however, and some students will inevitably recreate for themselves the crisis conditions to which they are accustomed. Postponed reading, consequently unprepared discussion; hasty, last-minute, gimmicky and superficial papers. Indolent distraction followed by unproductive frenzy. Since there are no grades to encourage self-deception, the student will usually recognize the unproductiveness of the pattern and will be troubled by it. As he tries to break out—*if* he tries—he is likely to discover how little he is master of himself. It is a lesson in the difficulty of freedom. He wants to; he resolves to; he tries to—but nothing happens. He cannot sit down or sit still; he cannot resist an invitation; a change in the weather and he is undone. Master of his fate and captain of his soul! A routine which makes the old habits pointless and which encourages and supports new and better ones is what the student needs. The external discipline makes sense only when it promotes self-discipline. It is a bridge between the old and the new—a necessary bridge.

The program has such a routine, but it is not foolproof. A student who lets it take over finds himself gradually working with more effectiveness and self-reliance and with a greater sense of power and freedom. We are not policemen, however, and a student who wants to play more familiar games can do so for a while until he either decides to try, or to leave, or until we decide he should be dropped. Resistance is utterly pointless and profitless, but it occurs anyway.

Individuality

All this talk of docility and discipline might suggest to the unwary that the program is a sort of boot camp designed to stamp out such vestiges of individuality as have survived the flattening effects of mass culture. This is not how it looks from the inside.

We cherish individuality and strengthen it. The common program, and the community of students and teachers it makes possible, is precisely the context in which individuality is revealed, encouraged, and developed. We are not a series of transient and sporadic classrooms. We are a working group of students and faculty who are closely related for a long time. We know each other. Our freshmen receive more faculty attention, on an individual basis, than do virtually all but the most fortunate graduate students. It is not a situation which demands or promotes uniformity.

The common program of reading, discussion, and writing serves as the background which heightens awareness of individual difference. It is only when we read and discuss the same thing, tackle the same task, that we discover how individual and different we are.

It is the same old story and one wearies of telling it. Polar notions involve each other; they do not destroy each other. "Change" is not a denial of "permanence"; "only the permanent changes." Sameness and difference, unity and multiplicity, public and private, individual and social—variations on the same theme. A collection of solipsistic eccentrics is not a collection of individuals. If you want individuals and individuality, create a community. Our students are unmistakably individuals.

We do, occasionally, get the echoes of a current generational slogan: "Don't let them get at your mind" (a polite version), and it has an ironic ring in an educational institution. But it is quite understandable. It is held that we are a sick society, that our good human nature has been corrupted and warped by bad social institutions and ideologies guarded by the established powers and propagated by the mass media and the servile school system; that most people, especially adults, have been tricked into taking absurd games seriously and behave with systematic insanity, moving through their destructive and joyless paces like zombies. A student who holds a version of this widespread and interesting view of things is also likely to think that he has, through accident, some "outside" help perhaps, and his own efforts, escaped or thrown over control. "They" (we) want to recapture him and will, if he does not guard it, invade his mind.

So he guards his mind and his hard-won and precarious individuality. Beleaguered and suspicious, he won't play. Sometimes he really won't, and there is nothing we can do except stand by patiently while he wanders through the faddish anti-establishment world looking for a home, starving the individuality he is trying to protect.

There are some games we refuse to play. "Solitaire" is one; "participatory democracy" is another. Each, in its own way, destroys the learning community which is the essence of the Experimental Program.

Relevance

What makes everything go, of course, is the curriculum, the ideas with which the program is involved. It dominates everything, and sustains us when we falter. I will discuss the curriculum more fully later, but here I wish to consider some general features of its relation to the life of the student.

The demand for "relevance" is hurled at the university in so many foolish ways that a self-respecting scholar may be tempted to dismiss it as an expression of self-centered impertinence, as misguided narrow-mindedness and short-sightedness. It is sometimes just that.

Many things are studied in the university which are not relevant to the war in Vietnam or the war in the ghetto or the war on poverty. The university is the kind of institution in which that sort of thing goes on and should go on. Whether the justification is that knowledge is an end in itself or that the strangest things turn out to be useful, we will, I am sure, resist any attempt to make immediate relevance to today's crises the test of whether something should be studied or taught, whether the attempt comes from economy-minded legislators or from crusading students.

More immediately annoying is the student who finds that the course he has enrolled in is "not relevant to him" and who seems to think that it should be made so at once. The professor is likely to think that the student should accommodate himself to the demands of the subject—not the other way around. "Irrelevant" sounds, sometimes, like "I'm bored," and only politeness keeps the professor from making the obvious replies.

But these unfortunate misuses only tend to discredit a concept whose legitimacy, at the lower-division level, must be recognized and honored. The graduate student who chooses to work for a degree in a particular field should expect to be required to show signs of becoming relevant to it. He, not the field, is on trial. To a lesser degree this holds also for the student pursuing the upper-division "major" of his choice. But the lower-division situation is quite different and the problem of relevance cannot be put aside.

We should consider what a freshman is. He is a person who has arrived at a crucial stage and is confronted with an array of incredibly difficult decisions which may set the pattern of his entire life. He has acquired or developed a set of ideas about the way the world is and about himself. These are of vital importance to him and to us, and they must be taken seriously.

I have already suggested that the entering student is, to a considerable degree, a creature of circumstance, and his ideas reflect the circumstance of intellectual and moral fashion. I have, elsewhere, given a caricature of the freshman philosophy of life and treated it as a bill presented to us as the belated price for the sins of the fathers. They are eating the grapes, and our teeth are set on edge.

They arrive with ideas, swinging between dogmatism and despairing uncertainty. We can systematically ignore the ideas or, if we know what we are doing, we can, in a special way, build the curriculum on them. That is what we must do, and that, in its proper sense, is what the demand for relevance is about.

To do this is not to pander to superficial interests but to respond appropriately to real needs. And we must do it our way, a way appropriate for a college, digging below the shrill level of fad and fashion to the bed-rock resources of our culture. If we try to do this, we discover that the great problems of today are, for the most part, the perennial problems in modern dress; and we discover also that the resources of the culture are far from depleted, archaic, or irrelevant. They are real resources, and if we use them properly we subject our own ideas to the kind of ordeal that constitutes education.

When I say that such a curriculum responds to real needs, I do not refer to the student's alone. They are the needs of the society as well. To the student, the question is, "What should I do with my life?" Before society answers, "Do this," or "Do that," or "Above all do as you're told" it had better take the occasion to ask aloud, "What are we up to?"

The lower division is the ground upon which these two questions meet and interact. Other things may intrude, but they are irrelevant. Scholars who are unwilling or unable to address themselves to these questions should, at least, stay out of the lower division. They are usurpers there, and if they have their way they displace the real curriculum and exile the big questions to the television talk show and the street-corner microphone.

One of the implications of this curricular conception is that the dominant perspective of the lower division is moral rather than scientific, normative rather than descriptive. The student is seen as an agent or a potential agent, and the organization of knowledge is shaped by relevance to action. "What should we do?" is the typical question in this perspective. It is a stage at which knowledge is instrumental to purpose. I have discussed elsewhere* the contrast between the normative-practical and the descriptive-predictive perspectives and the relevance of that distinction to the education of the political agent, the ruler, the citizen of a democratic polity—to "liberal education"—and I shall not retrace that argument here. It accounts, however, for the displacement of science, social as well as natural, from a central role in the lower-division curriculum. "What is to be done" takes precedence over "What is the case." This is a point of considerable controversy, and the argument is an easy one to lose in the university where the priorities seem quite different, and where the pursuit of knowledge, scientific or scholarly, organizes itself in its own terms and claims autonomy. It accounts, also, for the anomalous status of the lower division in the university structure. For it does not really share the primarily cognitive bent of the upper and graduate divisions. It is captive to them, however, and in its institutional weakness it suffers from the inroads and demands of the heedless and hard headed.

The moral perspective is, of course, the perspective of induction or initiation. It enters the quandary of the young student faced with the decisions of adjustment to, rejection of, or participation in the life of the society. It is the perspective which entertains *his* problems; it is also the perspective in which so-

* *Obligation and the Body Politic*, New York, 1960.

ciety solicits his full membership, explains its commitments, and invites his participation in its troubled but rewarding life.

It is a scene of wonderful confusion and misunderstanding, of mistaken and challenged identities. We think we are offering a generous invitation; he has heard of Greeks bearing gifts and looks the horse in the mouth. We take him to the mountain top and offer him power to turn deserts into gardens or offer wisdom in human affairs; we think he may have a divine nature; he thinks he hears a forked tongue and sees a cloven hoof—that we mean to turn gardens into deserts and take power over human beings. The commitment of membership in community is mistaken for bondage; slavery to desire and whim is mistaken for freedom.

We need to straighten it all out if we can. It is, no doubt, deplorable that the problem should arise. Where is the family? Where is the church? What has happened in the nursery school? What has become of the Boy Scouts? Alas! It is up to the college.

III. The Curriculum

Within the course system the problems of the curriculum are quite familiar—what collection of courses, what subjects, what order, what degree of concentration and diffusion, what required, what elective. The substitution of the program for the course does not eliminate all these considerations, but it drastically alters the context and form in which they appear. It brings the problem back to the teacher, to the teaching staff, as an integral part of his teaching activity. When the teacher gives a course he is responsible for its internal organization, but he can largely ignore the problem of inter-course or foreign relations. He may consider those problems as a member of his department or college, but he does not need to, except as they affect his own course. In the program the problems are internal and inescapable and go far beyond what is involved in the planning of a traditional course or course sequence.

The curriculum of the Experimental Program is, I believe, a meaningful and powerful one. It is a joy to the initiated and a stumbling block to the unsaved. Its principle of organization is difficult to express with clarity in familiar terms and appears subject to a host of academic questions and objections; and it seems, in addition to and also because of its organization, to pose insuperable teaching difficulties. I wish to explain its principles more clearly, and to explain away the difficulties if I can.

The principle which underlies everything and which creates most of the trouble is that the normal categories in which the university organizes knowledge and administers its pursuit are irrelevant to our purposes—to the purposes of first-program education—and should be ignored. We do not think in terms of "humanities" or "social science"; we do not even think in terms of "history" or "literature" or "political science" or "philosophy." It is not that we want to replace these categories with others. We do not quarrel with them; we simply do not use them, and, if they prescribe limits, we do not observe them. We read Homer, Thucydides, and Plato; but we do not say or think, "Now we are on literature," "Now we turn to history," "At last we come to philosophy."

These categories are quite legitimately the organizing categories of the university, of its schools, divisions, departments, and the faculty thinks of knowledge quite naturally in these terms. This makes communication somewhat baffling, and when we shrug off the politely proferred "interdisciplinary?" "integrated?" and mutter "No! Subdisciplinary," "A-disciplinary," incomprehension dawns. This is a university. Where does that fit in? The first difficulty, then, is that we do not use the normal categories.

A second and related difficulty is that we do not accept as a governing mission direct introduction to or preparation for the academic fields or disciplines which dominate the upper division and graduate programs. The first program comes before the second program, and our students, we know, will continue into the upper division and should be able to handle it. But there is an important sense in which we are not "introductory." Not in disciplinary terms.

This separates us from a whole tradition of lower-division curricular devices—the elements of X, an introduction to Y, a sampler survey of Z. And also from an interdisciplinary introduction to XY or an integrated introduction to division H. What else is there? Nothing, really, if we accept the conception of the lower division as essentially introductory, finding its *raison d'être* in the major and the graduate school. But we think the lower division has its own integrity and we resist the facile demand for "continuity" which only serves to facilitate and perpetuate the domination of the college by the graduate school. Not disciplinary, not introductory—unless it abdicates its real function and allows itself to become the neglected captive of the professionals.

I suppose this rejection of the academic discipline needs more explanation. A discipline is a way of studying something. What it studies is a particular aspect of a complex situation. The choice of aspect is definitive of the field, and the tools of the discipline are the techniques, skills, and practices appropriate for dealing with that aspect of things.

A man pauses in a public square to listen to someone speak. This is a crude macroscopic description of a fragment of what is going on at a moment of time in a particular place. A body is in motion, it has a chemical composition, glands are secreting, digestion, respiration, blood-pressure rises, languages, emotion, a political allegiance at stake, a moral crisis, an official mistake, lives take a different course, institutions tremble, a dozen histories take a sharp turn. How many aspects of this fragment of event can we describe or study? Physics, chemistry, biology, psychology, sociology, history, rhetoric, linguistics, political science, logic, ethics. Grist for all our mills.

Each discipline abstracts what concerns it and places it in its own context of classification, law, and explanation. Each has its own story to tell. There are many stories and most of them are probably true. An academic discipline is a sustained attempt to tell a particular kind of story—about poems or organizations, about very small things, very large things, short-lived or enduring, about warring, sheltering, growing, healing, trading, about people, animals, societies, rocks.

The ways we study and know the world reflect the structure of the university. The ways are varied, intensive, skillful, and, of course, specialized. No one has invented a better way, although we all have our particular complaints.

I do not quarrel with the conception that the upper-division experience for the student should be primarily that of catching a glimpse of the way things look from the perspective of one of the academic disciplines. Not only for what it shows him about the world but for what he learns about how "seeing" really goes on and about the significance of "seeing" for "doing." Nor, of course, do I quarrel generally with what the graduate school is up to. But what has all this got to do with the lower division?

The freshman is there to learn but not yet to learn to be a professional scholar. Some may become professionals, but that is only accidental. We can even encourage the choice later by those who show special fitness. But *that* is no more the aim of the lower division than it is the aim of hospitals to turn its patients into doctors. Putting it crudely, freshman courses— if we must have them—in literature, history, or philosophy should be conducted on the assumption that the student is going to be a dentist, stockbroker, or a civil servant, rather than a professor of literature, history, or philosophy.

What the freshman is going to become vocationally is really beside the point. He is already something that he will continue to be—a member of a society, a social individual, a center of values and awareness, a person required to act on our common stage. He needs to get his bearings there so that, if he doesn't wander off, he can understand the part he is to play.

So we come again to the perspective of the agent and its problems as shaping the lower-division curriculum, not the perspective of the academic discipline and its problems. That is why the first program is neither disciplinary nor introductory.

There are two aspects of the first-program curriculum which need consideration. First, the problem of shaping, forming, or constructing a particular curriculum without the familiar disciplinary guidelines; second, the problem of competence to teach such a curriculum when the teacher himself is where he is because of his own training and expertise in a discipline.

If our general thesis is accepted, the purpose of the first program is to lead the student into a broad and sustained examination of the "moral" dimensions of the situation in which he and we find ourselves. The curriculum is a concrete plan for doing that. Let me present some preliminary assumptions underlying the Experimental Program's curriculum or, perhaps, its search for a curriculum.

First, it must be related to the deep controversial issues of our time. This is not to say that it is about current events or that we even necessarily deal with the problems in the language and temper of current controversy. This particular war is concrete and unique. But it is also an exemplification or instance of war, and the problems it poses are not unique. Conscience confronts law in a particular circumstance today, but the terms of that confrontation are ancient and familiar. To understand our situation requires not only that we be acquainted with it in its concrete particularity but that we see it also as an instance of a kind of situation. We must study *our* problems; but not always or necessarily in current terms.

Second, the program is primarily reflective rather than experiential. Our concern is with gaining understanding rather than with gaining experience. It is temptingly easy to misunderstand this point. We recognize the complex interdependence of understanding and experience, the need to have real examples to think about, the need to attach understanding to what we are living through. But it is a matter of emphasis and timing. The student comes to us already overwhelmed by experience he is struggling to understand. He is soon involved in the exciting and broadening life of the modern university community. He will graduate to half a century of active life in the world of events and actions. We believe that his time in the program is best spent in the program, not in the world. Our curriculum is, without apology, bookish, not activist.

It is difficult to discuss the "construction" of a curriculum. There is no recipe for putting one together. I think the reason is that "construct" and "put together" convey the wrong impression. A curriculum is a work of art. It is based on an inspiration, and its history is the working out of that inspiration in appropriate forms. As with other works of art, a curriculum can be subjected to the process of analysis and criticism; we can discern its structure and come, perhaps, to understand the basis of its power; we can learn to develop effective variations and modifications. But the process of analysis and dissection, of appreciation and justification, is not to be confused with the process of creation. Making up a game, and describing and appreciating it, are two quite different things.

We are not swamped with first-program curricular inspirations. The standard lower division is a distinctly uninspired habit, and apart from it there are few candidates. St. John's rests on an inspiration. There is a cluster of institutions living on the student-interest-centered unstructured "happening" inspiration. Perhaps something more, but the field is thin. The Experimental Program lives on the inspiration of Alexander Meiklejohn's Athens-America curriculum, established for a brief time at Wisconsin in the 1920's. We have our own variation—we are captivated, not enslaved—but the Meiklejohn conception was there from the very beginning. Without it, in fact, the Experimental Program would not have been created.

I am now convinced that a dominating idea must come first. Without it nothing happens. This has some implications for first-program curricular planning and educational reform. It means, I think, that we should expect nothing, or very little, from academic committees, commissions, or task forces, in the way of real innovation or reform. They are, at best, midwives; they may encourage fertility and even help with delivery, but they neither conceive nor bear. Nor can we simply bring together a small group of faculty members and ask them to work out and teach a first program. Unless they are already all dominated by a common conception the faculty will either fall apart or will work out a compromise or *modus vivendi*. They may put something together, but it will not have much life.

The first-program curriculum, in short, cannot be simply put together. It must grow out of a simple idea and be developed by a group committed to the idea. The heart of the program "constitution," of which I spoke earlier, is the commitment of the faculty to its governing inspiration.

But if there are not very many distinctive first-program curricular ideas around, we do not, on the other hand, need very many, and there is no need to be discouraged by the relative infrequency of radical curricular inspiration. A few basic conceptions given institutional form can serve as models to be adopted, imitated, or modified. Creation is difficult; intelligent imitation and modification will serve the ends of education.

What is required, therefore, is not a handbook on how to invent programs, but an analysis of a program in being. We think that our curriculum is successful, that it is not dependent upon any of the peculiarities of our university (in fact the distinctive character of the university at Berkeley creates only added difficulties and obstacles), and that it is easily adaptable and adoptable.

The starting point was Meiklejohn's Athens-American conception—a two-year integrated program focusing, the first year, on the Greeks, the second year, on America. We did not try it quite in that form. A whole year on Greece seemed a little too much, and seventeenth-century England—the Puritan revolution —had some special attraction, so we divided the first year between Greece and England. For the second year, we planned to begin with the period of the constitutional convention in America and end with the contemporary scene.

The program as it was presented for approval thus seemed to have four segments. Each segment was full of crisis and turmoil, and we succumbed to the temptation to describe the program as a study of culture in crisis—four different crises, four different periods, apparently a peculiar "historical" approach.

We bore with cheerful indifference the criticisms that since we settled on crises we were "teaching revolution" and that for a "historical" program we had some strange gaps.

Our preliminary description was far from satisfactory, and by degrees we shifted emphasis from periods to problems or issues or themes. But if we said "war and peace" or "freedom and authority" we had not yet accounted for our doing it in this way. It is not a bad formulation and perhaps it will do as well as any as long we are restrained by modesty or by fear of uproarious and unextinguishable laughter from stating what is closer to the real case—that we have hit upon, in manageable form and extent, a rich version of the basic moral curriculum of our culture.

The Greeks constitute for us a great exemplary episode. Its dramatic center is the Peloponnesian War seen through the eyes of Thucydides. But everything we read illuminates that tragedy. Homer is in the background, Aeschylus, Sophocles, Euripides are brooding commentators, Plato reaps its lesson. It is an unparalleled chorus for the basic human plot. We echo it in everything we do. It is the great introduction to ourselves.

We do not really care about the seventeenth century after all, exciting and crucial as it is. It happens to be where we pick up the other great cultural strand of our lives. It gives us the King James Bible, Shakespeare, Hobbes, and Milton—the Judeo-Christian tradition in a strain especially constitutive of the American tradition and character.

As for America, we take the covenant, the Constitution, the law, and the court, the living complex institution, as the thread which guides us in the attempt to understand what we are up to. We have followed this thread haltingly but we will persist with growing confidence. We are the people of the law if we are anything.

This is the structure of our curriculum—an episode, a strand, an institution. It is deep and varied, fundamental, relevant, and even cumulative.

It is possible, I suppose, to substitute another episode for the Greek one. I doubt if anyone who knows it will be tempted to do so. It is possible to pick up the Judeo-Christian tradition in another way, but the cost in loss of fringe benefits would be high. It is possible to reject law as the center of the American year, but also at a sacrifice. Tinkering is allowed, and we may even do some ourselves. But it is great as it stands; and within it, as it stands, there is a good deal of flexibility.

To the charge that this is all Western provincial and that a citizen of the modern world needs to know a "foreign" culture, we have a standard two-part answer. Our real culture is a foreign culture to most of us; and, you cannot understand a foreign culture if you do not understand your own.

To the charge that it leaves out too much of importance even in our own cultural tradition, the reply must be that, of course, it leaves out much. There is no alternative. We cannot include everything. If we try we end up scurrying frantically and hopelessly through masses of material, without enjoyment and without understanding. We must select carefully and be ruthless in rejecting great things.

I turn now from the problem of the construction of the curriculum to the questions of its teachability. However attractive a curriculum might appear, if it cannot be "taught" or if professors cannot be found to teach it, or are unqualified to meet its challenge, it isn't of much use. Let me first marshall the standard objections.

The program violates the first principle of university teaching: an expert should teach what he is expert in. The good faculty member of a good university is a man who has taken a particular branch of knowledge as his province, who has become a specialist capable of contributing to the advancement of knowledge. He knows more than anyone else around about his part of his field. When he teaches he should teach what he knows, communicate his special insights. Thus, his teaching goes hand in hand with his other work and is not entirely a distraction. At the same time, the student can be assured that he is getting his information or his particular training from a certified source. Teaching by experts; learning from experts. That is the rock upon which university teaching and learning rests.

But the curriculum of the program neglects the use of our assets, it ignores expertise. It ranges from epic through tragedy and history and philosophy, from ancient to modern, from the poet to the judge. The same staff teaches everything and most of the time the teacher is out of his field. Even if he is willing, he will need to prepare himself, and that means a decision to put aside "his own work" as a scholar. It is a full-time involvement, so he drops out of the race for several years. Scholarship suffers, his career suffers, and the student gets some amateur teaching. It makes no sense.

Of course, there may be some people around who would like to teach in such a program. Scholars who have tired of scholarship or become bored with their fields and want to 'teach.' They are usually gambles the university has lost. They might be happy as 'generalists' teaching in the lower division. But the true scholar belongs in his classroom or seminar teaching what he really knows. And even if he would want to, he cannot really know what the program curriculum requires him to know well enough to teach it. And anyway, a proper selection of courses will give the student everything he could get in the program—and expertly taught.

This is the standard barrage. It sounds formidable, and it is. "Barrage" is perhaps the wrong word. It is the siren song and who, in the university, does not hear it without longing? Knowledge, certainty, security, an unchallengeable status, a tight little island, a chosen few, a mine of one's own, digging, finding, eureka! I confess I hear it too and am sorely tempted. . . . Well, warm the wax to stop the ears, get tied to the mast, issue strict orders; row on.

The question of expertise is intrinsically related both to the kind of materials or books which make up the curriculum and to the kind of use we make of them. A discussion of these matters will, I think, put the problem of expertness in a different light.

We read great books, classics, masterpieces, and very little else. If we deny that we are a "Great Books Program" it is because we do not use the selective and organizing principles, and perhaps do not share the educational and metaphysical assumptions which have come to be associated with the Great Books Program. But we prefer great books to lesser books.

This is not simply an innocent preference for high quality. The classic (as I shall loosely call it) that we read has some important features beyond the fact that it is a great achievement of mind and art. Quite simply, a classic escapes from or transcends its generative context. It retains its intelligibility and significance when it is taken out of context. It is self-contained, a world of its own. Like a pearl, it can gain from its setting, but its best setting is not its oyster, and it really cannot even be said to belong there.

I am not saying that a classic is not evoked by the situation, that it does not use the materials at hand, that it is not, in its time, timely. But its response to what evokes it is a response at a level deeper than the current surface of things. If it stays on the surface it is gone with the surface and to read it later requires that we reconstruct what is gone. But if it is deeper, it takes us, when we read it, below our own surface to the common bedrock level. The historical context may explain some things about it, but the classic is fundamentally intelligible and significant without it. It is not a period piece.

You do not have to know anything about Greece or about Plato in order to read and understand and enjoy the *Republic*. It does not need background. You can read and enjoy *King Lear* without knowing anything about Shakespeare or his England. A reading of the work may produce an interest in its genesis, and what we discover if we pursue that interest may contribute to our understanding. It may also distract us, and if we shift our attention to the context we may well impair our experience and appreciation of the work itself. If we must commit the genetic fallacy at least let us not commit it prematurely.

This is a controversial point, but I shall not push it. I have said enough to indicate that the program's use of the classic is not "historical." We are more concerned with the truth or validity of an idea than with its history. Whether Plato is right in what he says about show business is more important than why he happened to say it. More important to us, at this stage of the game.

But besides being detachable from its historical context, the classic is not dependent upon the various disciplinary contexts in which the university is prone to place it. Plato's *Republic*, let us say, belongs to the philosophy department, and there it takes its place in the field of philosophy, preceded by the pre-Socratics, followed by Aristotle, related this way to Hegel, that way to Plotinus, the fountainhead of this movement, the whipping boy of that. For "philosophy" the *Republic* may shrink to the "divided line" and "the form of the good" with much of the rest passed over as of no special philosophical interest. What is left over, other departments can have. Or consider the *Iliad*. It is in Greek so it belongs to the Greek department. It is an epic so it probably belongs also to comparative literature or to whoever takes all epics as his province. To study it is to take it in that context, subject to the categories of that discipline. Every professor belongs to a department, every department has its field, and everything we read "belongs" in one or more fields. For us to "teach" a book is to seem to invade a field without a license, to commit academic trespass.

But the classic escapes simple "belonging" in a disciplinary context. It can be put there, but it need not be. Its author was not a member of the union or discipline which studies his work. He did not write his book for professors, however confidently they appropriate it. I do not really quarrel with the appropriation for purposes of disciplinary scholarship and study. No doubt it must be done. I quarrel with the arrogance of the appropriator who thinks that because he is interested in tusks the elephant belongs entirely to him. I doubt if the tusk collector appreciates elephants the way we do.

A glance at our reading list will quickly reveal that whatever we read is independent of both the historical and the disciplinary context. It can be confronted directly. It is readable, "non-technical," and without gratuitous complexity. It does not require the mediation of the historian or the disciplinary expert.

Of course we do not read a series of discrete and unrelated classics. We develop a sustaining context of our own. We begin cold, with the *Iliad,* but everything after that is read in a steadily thickening context of insights, questions, ideas. One of the delights of the program is the growing sense of relation and interconnection as we progress. Each book seems to strike a note which reveals a new pattern or develops a familiar one. What we once read is always with us, and everything seems to get related to everything else. The unity of the program is the real context of each work, as the melody is the context of the note.

The point of this discussion of the relation of what we read in the program to the historical and disciplinary contexts is that the usual forms of university expertise are irrelevant to teaching in the program. It does not require expertness in the particular books we study. It requires of the teacher intelligence, the ability to read, and some understanding of the teaching process.

There is really no mystery about it. Let me illustrate what is involved.

We come to Hobbes's *Leviathan*. We have already read the Greeks, including Thucydides' History (which Hobbes admired and translated into English). *Leviathan* appeared in 1651. Hobbes was a refugee from revolution and civil war. He is responding to the turmoil and destruction England was experiencing. There is no doubt about that. But he analyzes, diagnoses, and prescribes in general terms. What shall we make of *Leviathan*? Do we need to know about the civil war? About James and Charles? About Parliament and Pym and Wentworth and Cromwell? It is interesting and it does no harm if we know something. But it does not help very much, and it is, above all, not necessary. The general statements Hobbes makes about the causes of conflict and about what is necessary for peace constitute a coherent argument. If we want to "apply" it to a concrete situation, to test it against examples, we do not need to use *his* situation or *his* examples. We do not need to try to acquire information about the seventeenth century—although we can if we wish and someday we may wish to—in order to test Hobbes's theses. We can place his theory in the context of our day, our conflicts, our attempts at remedies. This will not only test his theory more effectively than it would be tested by our feeble, second-hand knowledge of the seventeenth century, it will also help us understand our own situation better—whether we agree with Hobbes or not. We can, in short, free the *Leviathan* from its seventeenth-century context and dip it into ours. Its relevance is then inescapable.

Again, *Leviathan* is the third attempt Hobbes made to write on this subject. For a student of Hobbes the successive shifts in formulation are exciting and illuminating. Should we not read *De Cive* as well? Trace the development? Look at his other works? The answer, I am sure, is "no!" We are not that interested in Hobbes. (Some of us are, it so happens, "professional" students of Hobbes, and we are interested; but the *program* is not, and we need to restrain our private passion.) *Leviathan* is more than enough for us, and it stands on its own feet. We do not need to read something else first.

And again, Hobbes is a figure in the history of political theory. Do we need to know how he fits into that story? How he is related to Locke and Rousseau, to Bodin and Grotius, to Aristotle and St. Thomas? No, we do not; not now.

There is really no escape. We must simply read *Leviathan*. Why the struggle? It is better than anything written about it. It is clear, powerful, imaginative, beautifully written. To read it, as Hobbes would say, is to "read oneself." Are we like that? Is that what we must do? Can't we get out of it?

The book itself, the context of the program, the context of our own day—that is what is essential. What does he say? Is he right? These are the questions.

Let us consider another example, a different kind of book, the *Iliad*. What are we to do with it? As usual, there are a number of fascinating things we do not do. The poetry? Not really, in translation, although we are grateful to Lattimore. The Homeric question? She remains a mystery to us. The structure of the epic? The oral question—can a Jugoslavian bard really do it? Was there a Troy where someone said he found it? Was Odysseus a bear, or a Jew? When did it happen? Who monkeyed with the catalogue of ships? What can we infer from the description of the cap worn on the raid and the judgment scene on the shield of Achilles, the lump of iron given for a prize, the human slaughter on the pyre? We do not pursue such questions. We are not that lucky.

We try to read the *Iliad*. What do we find? First, a human city: walls, shrines, homes, fathers, mothers, children, husbands, wives, an inner order, a way of life. Opposed to it a line of beached ships: an expedition, men on a mission, leaders, followers, comrades, rivals, mixed motives in a common cause. Between the city and the ships, a field of war, a scene of courage, fear, strength, weakness, weariness, endurance, and poignant, brutal death.

Why are they there? For Helen? To recapture and hold elusive beauty? To restore one shattered home by destroying another? To honor treaties? To satisfy ambition, to win glory and loot? Why does Troy fight? Must it defend its errant son? Does it harbor injustice? Is it the innocent victim of aggression?

They are caught up in war. They are tired of it. They want to stop, but cannot. So the destruction goes on, and in its course we see it touch almost every possible human relation, evoke every emotion, test every character. In camp, city, and field we see humanity at war, helplessly destroying and weeping. Homer may nod, but he misses very little.

We live with the *Iliad* for a few weeks. The strangeness wears off. A terrible question creeps up on us. Has anything changed? Are *we* still on the plain before Troy? That is how we begin.

What discipline? What expertise? The only problem is to learn how to read, to let Homer in. That is difficult enough. Not reading words, but reading a mind. The fact is that reading is, today, a highly undeveloped art. There is a good deal of justified complaint about student writing, but student reading is probably worse, and the deficiency is more serious. It is almost enough if the faculty can teach students how to read.

This discussion of the classic nature of our curricular material and of the way we read it is an oblique response to the charge that the program violates the university principle: "experts teach what they are expert in." The charge is only partially admitted. The program does not follow that rule in its ordinary sense. But we do not violate that principle in the sense of using non-experts to do what experts should be doing. Ordinary university disciplinary expertise is simply not called for. It is not relevant to what we should be doing. The program is not a place where experts *can* teach what they are expert in.

The question, then, is not whether the university should tolerate a program which violates its formal teaching principle, but whether it should tolerate and even support a program to which the principle does not apply. Or, to put it another way, the question is whether the lower division belongs in the university at all.

If my general argument is sound, there is real curricular discontinuity between the first program and the other two programs. The discontinuity is great enough to enable us to face the question of administrative and even physical separation with equanimity. The association is a peculiar one. The first program, the lower division, does not need the university and is not intellectually dependent on it—although it is subservient. The university gets all the benefits. If it lets it do its job it gets better educated students. And when it does not let it do its real work it uses it as a recruiting ground and preparatory school for its own professional concerns. It is grudging, predatory, and ungrateful. The lower division would be better off on its own. But the university community would be poorer without it. In spite of everything the lower division is the only civilizing influence it has left. Without it the university is only a glorified trade school.

But the concrete problem, as long as the first program retains its position as part of the university, is that of getting the university faculty to undertake the teaching of the first-program curriculum. My only concrete suggestion is the combination of a permanent core staff and greater attention to the professors' first-program readiness. This may not be enough. But the curriculum, at any rate, is teachable.

The program, its curriculum, is suitable for anyone and everyone faced with the necessity of living his life in today's world. It will, of course, not be available to everyone, and we enjoy the principle of toleration which allows us to exist as one of the many options which should be available to entering students. Since it is unlikely that we will be able, immediately, to solve the staffing problem in a way which would support more than very limited expansion, I will not push the argument that every freshman should enter, or be required to enter, a program like ours. The practical limitations make it unnecessary to grapple with some bad arguments.

The program would be good for everyone and probably especially good for those who are least likely to choose it. If the lower division is terminal for many students they would be infinitely better off in the program than if they wander through the standard collection of introductory courses, and many of them might discover that they are not terminal after all. Students "who know what they want to be," and who are required to devote their lower-division years largely to technical preparation for the major deserve sympathy. They cannot fit the program in, although they need it. Some of the sciences are the worst offenders in this respect, but it is unlikely that they will do anything about it. They are too strong to move, and they are full of reasons why it is necessary for the entering freshman who wants to be an X to immediately take this and that and the other. They are sorry about it and wish someone would whip up a nice compact liberal education which their students could swallow in their spare time. They are, I think, in more of a hurry than they need to be; but they probably think not.

The curriculum, incidently, is not only good for students. It is an educational experience for the faculty, and if we all took a hand in teaching it we might rediscover what "academic community" means.

To sum up, the first-program curriculum is easier to teach than to construct. It is not the introductory stage of training in the academic disciplines; its orientation and perspective is "moral." The material is "classic" and its proper use does not involve the ordinary academic expertise. It is, in principle, good for everybody. It is about, and it cultivates, freedom. It should probably be required for everyone, but we are neither institutionally nor intellectually ready for that.

Conclusion

A sustained attempt to improve the quality of education reveals, as perhaps nothing else does, how deeply we, as a society, are imbued with the ideas and attitudes of competitive individualism. We do not really think of man as a political animal or even understand what that means. We think of him as essentially a private person created, by God or by himself, complete with mind, self, goals, rights—autonomous and naturally sovereign over himself. All relations are foreign relations, entered into for private reasons, justified in private terms. Even when these ideas get shaken the attitudes persist, and we prefer patching up the worn spots with a sentimentality in which we do not really believe to giving up the old familiar ideas. We are attached to the weapons with which we have fought and won some earlier battles. Even our misconceptions, we think, have served us well, and it seems safer to cling to them than to risk "philosophy."

So we remain individualists. Children of the polis, we deny our generative source and then enjoy our crisis of identity. We search for ourselves in all the wrong places.

We are, characteristically, uneasy and ambivalent about the exercise of the teaching power. On the one hand, we have created a system of public education on an unprecedented scale; on the other hand, we are extremely reluctant to face the implications of this massive "governmental" involvement in the shaping of individual mind and character. We believe, apparently, that if we don't think about what we are doing we are safe; to even *describe* what we do seems "totalitarian." Government (the school?) is to leave the mind of the individual alone, although, of course, it should eradicate racism and all that sort of thing. Salvation is another empire to be acquired in a fit of absent-mindedness.

The relation of society and government to the mind of the citizen is the most crucial and neglected of problems. This is not the place to pursue the subject, but we can stand a passing reminder about democracy and freedom.

Democracy is not anarchy; it is an organized and complex way of life, and it requires the cultivation of its appropriate state of mind. That state of mind, which alone can sustain the institutions of democracy, does not develop naturally or by neglect. The democratic nature is also a "second nature" and it needs deliberate nurturing. To be committed to democracy is to give a special mandate and a special character to the school and college.

Freedom is the fruit of the successful operation of the teaching power. Freedom is power and it, too, must be deliberately cultivated. It rests on discipline, not whim; on habit, not impulse; on understanding, not desire. It is a difficult achievement.

The American college today betrays its function if it does not take its democratic tutelary and initiatory tasks seriously. In cultivating freedom, the college can neither abandon the student's mind to its own devices nor abdicate to him the responsibility for creating or administering the conditions conducive to his own growth. At these points, as at others, we see the doctrines of individualism playing havoc with the spirit and operation of constructive institutions of growth and liberation, dooming us to a life of change through weakness and conflict rather than through strength and understanding.

The university, enterprising in the pursuit of knowledge, is a stronghold of individualism. But its own distinctive problems have not been my concern here. I have touched on the university only as it distorts and destroys the college. It has been a Procrustean host, and the college sleeps uneasily in its embrace.

The college itself, especially the lower division, needs fundamental reconstruction. But it is firmly set in its joyless ways and, under current pressures, is likely to drift in the wrong direction. The faculty, which alone can save it, is, regrettably, the vested interest most difficult to move. It acts out of conviction and habit, but what it has created and what it maintains is in educational, social, and human terms a disastrous failure.

The Experimental Program has attacked the problem root and branch. It has shown that there is another and a better way. The only question is whether it can survive and grow against the inertia of prevailing institutions.

The prospect is not hopeless. The task is not, at this point, to effect a total conversion of any particular college to the first-program pattern. It is, rather, to gain an exemplary foothold wherever possible. There is really no reason why every community college or junior college, every four-year college or university—public or private—could not, within a short time, have a first-program unit in operation. Every institution has at least the necessary handful of faculty who could do it, and that is all it would take. It is not expensive or elaborate or cranky.

If the program can gain foothold for fair trial it will prove itself in many ways. It may even turn out that sanity and joy are contagious.

PART TWO

This section consists of two reports which show the Experimental Program in the process of taking shape. The first, written after the first turbulent year, expresses the initial conception of the program, describes our initial attempt at developing a pattern of activity, and reveals the points at which we met with unexpected difficulties and disappointments.

The second report drafted during the middle of the third year, describes and explains the modifications in the program and tries, to some extent, to place the program in a broader context of institutional analysis and social theory.

First Report to the Faculty, September 1966

The Experimental Collegiate Program has now been in existence for a year. While it is certainly too early to speak with any confidence of its results, an informal interim report to the Berkeley faculty seems appropriate.

I

The program is a direct spiritual decendant of the Experimental College created and conducted at the University of Wisconsin by Alexander Meiklejohn in the 1920's. Dr. Meiklejohn was, in fact, a sympathetic observer of the early stages of the development of the Berkeley variation.

A number of problems had to be solved before the program could come into operation. The University at Berkeley is a powerful, complex institution with a large, vigorous student body and a large, confident faculty. Over many years programs and patterns of study have burgeoned, reflecting many educational conceptions and needs; and general educational requirements and standards have been embodied in university legislation. A new program had not only to be approved on its academic merits but students in such a program had to come to terms with college and university requirements. The winning of academic sanction was seen from the beginning as the major problem. Unless the faculty authorized the program there would be no program.

Apart from academic sanction the problems involved teaching staff, budget, and space. Faculty members willing and eager to take part in the program had to be freed from their departmental responsibilities for one or two years. Funds had to be provided on rather short notice. And space had to be found in a situation in which space is very scarce.

In retrospect, the launching difficulties do not seem to have been very great. But since there have been rumors of war and, no doubt, some misunderstandings, a brief account may be useful.

In the late spring of 1964 (before the Free Speech Movement had appeared on the scene) the proposal, in rough form, was taken informally to President Clark Kerr. He responded with friendly enthusiasm, and we were encouraged by the knowledge that there was support at the highest administrative level.

Early in the fall of 1964 the proposal was taken to Dean

William B. Fretter of the College of Letters and Science. He was sympathetic and open minded, made some helpful concrete suggestions, and sketched out the path leading to academic approval. This involved several meetings with the Dean and the Executive Committee of the College—augmented by the chairmen of several other committees. The presentation was largely oral, and we were not pressed to write out more than a brief two-page statement of the plan.

The first serious check was at the hands of the College Committee on Courses. Normally, a new course is proposed by a department, and the Committee exercises some quality and jurisdictional control. And normally a course is about something which can be stated fairly clearly and carries about three units of credit. We requested approval for a two-year program without courses, which we were calling, for accounting purposes, a 48-unit "course." It is not surprising or shocking that the Committee declined to approve such a course on the basis of the brief description provided.

It was also clear, however, that we could not, at that stage, provide more detail. The details were still to be worked out by the teaching staff which was ready to take up the work should the proposal be approved. We were in no position—nor really willing—to attempt a speculative mock-up of a sample semester.

At this point a closer look at university legislation revealed that the College of Letters and Science had been authorized by the Academic Senate to conduct experimental programs for a limited period of time simply on the recommendation of the Executive Committee and with the approval of the faculty of the College. The Executive Committee recommended approval and, at a rather sparsely attended meeting, the faculty gave its approval.

There is, however, a Berkeley Division Committee on Courses, and, out of habit, the proposal was routinely sent to it. Like its corresponding committee of the College of Letters and Science, it also was unwilling to give its approval without much more information. This appeared fatal. Spring vacation was upon us, and everything else waited upon academic authorization. It was almost too late for the fall of 1965, and a year's delay was, for various reasons, out of the question. We were rescued from this impasse by a ruling of the Committee on Rules and Jurisdiction that the approval of the Faculty of the College of Letters and Science was, under existing legislation, all the approval needed.

The legacy of the encounters with the Committees on Courses was an unfortunate one. While we were duly and properly authorized, nevertheless, the fact that we had by-passed or overridden the course committees subjected us to suspicion and criticism.

With academic authorization achieved, we turned to other problems. Acting Chancellor Martin Meyerson, though heavily pressed by problems growing out of the FSM, gave us his full support. Professors Albert Bendich, Norman Jacobson, Anthony Ostroff, Samuel Schaaf, and Joseph Tussman were given departmental leaves; a budget was pieced together; and after almost coming to grief in the quest for space we were given the use of a recently vacated old fraternity house on the edge of the campus.

In July, a brief description of the program was sent to all who had been admitted to Berkeley as freshmen with an invitation to apply for admission if interested. It was clearly stated that the program was not an "honors" program. We received about 325 applications and admitted 150 (75 men, 75 women) selected randomly.

During the summer the faculty planned and prepared itself for the first year's work. In September—somewhat to our astonishment—students arrived and we were off!

The lesson is fairly clear: a large, complex university can indeed be flexible and receptive to innovation. The administration proved to be, at every level, helpful and sustaining. Although its powers of initiative in this area are slight it does not see itself—and it is not—hostile to change. As for the faculty—it is, of course, the great conservative force on the educational scene. The practices of the institution largely express faculty views and attitudes. There is no doubt but that at essential points the conceptions embodied in the Experimental Collegiate Program run counter to deeply held convictions about scholarship and teaching. Realizing this, we are grateful for the patience, tolerance, and good humor with which the faculty at Berkeley has authorized us to take liberties with established practice.

II

The graduate, the upper-division, and the lower-division teaching situations present the university with distinctive tasks and challenges. Graduate education is, essentially, professional training; we are initiating relatively mature students into our own guilds, providing for the continuity and development of our own academic disciplines. At the upper-division level we are also working close to our professional concerns. For the upper division is characterized, even dominated, by the conception of the "major." While the major is, of course, preparation for graduate work it is not, in principle, only that. We deem it an important part of the general A.B. program that a student pursues understanding under the aegis of one of the academic disciplines, in sufficient depth so that he can grasp something of the methods, the spirit, the central concepts, and the problems which characterize it. We do not consider the major as "wasted" on those who do not pursue graduate work in the field. At both the graduate and upper-division levels the faculty is working "professionally" and teaches with interest and confidence. But the lower division, for which our program is designed, presents a radically different picture. Commitment to a vocational path is generally being deferred. It is, of course, a time of preparation, but it is in many ways more significantly the culmination of earlier phases of education, a time of orientation and reorientation. There is no "major" in the lower division, and we try (often unsuccessfully) to guard against premature specialization.

The lower division is the only phase of university education during which the student is not primarily under the authority of a department. Nevertheless, his education—the courses he takes—are offered by departments. And while the departments may not necessarily be overconcerned with recruiting (or seducing) for their disciplines, it is inevitably the case that lower-division courses tend to be—explicitly or not—"introductions to" or "elements of" an academic discipline.

A department, after all, represents a discipline. Faculty members are members of departments. Their status, their competence, is essentially disciplinary, and the more university-like or graduate-school- or research-oriented the institution the more will this be the case. Faculty members are chosen for excellence or the promise of excellence in a particular field, and when they do what they do best they are working at and within the discipline. This is description, not criticism. But the result is that the lower division is the spiritual stepchild of the university. It is conducted by departments which, on the whole, have their minds on something else.

It is not our purpose here to provide another exhaustive analysis of the defects of the lower division. Everyone is aware that something goes wrong. It is not entirely the fault of the curriculum, but something we do, or fail to do, contributes to the sophomore slump, to disillusionment, to alienation and bitterness. It is widely recognized that our entering students are very good. They have been under heavy pressure, and their preparation is better than it used to be. They are prepared for hard work and concerned about serious matters. The student, in short, is not the problem.

It is against this all-too-familiar background that we present this interim report on the theory and practice of the Experimental Program. And we stress, at the outset, that, in addressing ourselves to the lower-division situation we are taking for granted the value of the disciplinary way of life incarnated in the upper-division conception of the "major." What we are trying is a different way of handling the first two years.

Stated negatively, our problem is to provide an alternative to the system of sampling introductions to the academic disciplines as the organizing principle of the first two years. We are not disciplinary; nor are we interdisciplinary. We are non-disciplinary or sub-disciplinary. Our position, with all the difficulties it entails, is that lower-division education need not, should not, be conceived in terms of the academic professions.

If this is taken seriously, other familiar notions get shaken. Consider "subject." A subject is something a professor has, even when he does not have problems. It is a purely academic category—a subdivision of a field over which a department holds precarious and sometimes exclusive jurisdiction. And a "course" is simply a crude administrative device for teaching a subject. Quite naturally, "taking courses" has gotten confused with "getting an education."

But apart from this passing suggestion that there may be some deep and subtle connections between "courses," "subjects," and "academic disciplines," a difficulty with courses is that the student is taking four or five of them at the same time. And it is clear that this involves a fragmentation of attention and energy and very little in the way of coherence or unity. So, taking a firm grip on the baby, we throw out the course and plan the semester (or quarter) as a whole without internal division into courses or subjects.

It is not easy to make our organizing principle explicit, although, in fact, we think it worked out beautifully. It is easy to say that each semester is focused on a particular period— fifth-century Greece, seventeenth-century England—but that may suggest more historical concern than we really had. We picked these periods (and we could easily have selected others instead) because they produced a rich and varied literature in which powerful minds grappled with fundamental human problems. So that "problem-centered" is perhaps as adequate a characterization as "period-centered." But we defined the problem rather loosely, if at all. We sometimes said of the first semester that the question was, "Why did the Greeks destroy themselves in the Peloponnesian Wars?" But we really did not try to answer it in any careful or systematic way. It hovered usefully as "a brooding omnipresence in the sky." For both semesters the reading list is more revealing than any abstract statement of the organizing principle.

Educational form has two aspects: first, the formulation and development of the intellectual theme or themes; and second the development of a fruitful habit or pattern of work involving reading and writing, lecture and discussion. And just as we were breaking away from the traditional subject and course, so were we also breaking with the conventional classroom and examination pattern.

The problem was this: we had five senior faculty members working full time in the program and 150 students. This 30-1 ratio was mitigated by the addition of five teaching assistants. How could the available teaching energy be brought to bear so as best to further the educational life of the student? We expected to make use of the whole range of devices—from lectures to the entire group to individual conference—although some things were clear from the start. There was a place for the lecture, but we did not dream of approaching the 10 to 12 hours a week which 12 units would normally involve. There was an important place for the individual conference or tutorial but our student-faculty ratio precluded regular or routine individual tutorial instruction. In accepting the 30-1 ratio we understood that we were not to attempt an individual tutorial system of instruction.

The formal structure for the first year was as follows: We designated Tuesday as lecture day and asked each student to keep the hours ten to twelve and two to four free from outside commitments. We expected to have a rather full day: possibly two hours of lecture in the morning (staff or visitor) followed by discussions in groups of thirty from two o'clock to three, reassembling at three for further lecture, panel, or general discussion. The first semester we also reserved Friday afternoon, two to four, for additional lectures.

In addition, each student was to attend a seminar, in groups of fifteen, for a two-hour period once each week.

Thus, the formal schedule for the student involved up to four hours of meeting on Tuesday, an occasional additional lecture Friday afternoon or during an evening, and a two-hour seminar. Attendance was required in principle and was somewhat sporadic in practice. We expected that there would be a great deal of informal group meeting and discussion at the house.

We also planned that the student would write a paper every two or three weeks and would, from time to time, have a conference about his work with a faculty member or a teaching assistant. There was also a "term project."

The faculty members' schedule shaped up as follows: he participated in or attended all Tuesday exercises. He had two seminars each week. He read student papers, conferred with students about papers or other work, held general office hours, was sometimes available for evening discussions at the house, spent several hours in staff conference and, in addition, studied the same material the students were studying.

So far as we allowed ourselves to dream of "community" it was seen in these terms: a common intellectual enterprise, a common attempt at understanding through grappling with the same problems through the same material. There was no "course" to be given or taken. Everything turned on the students' becoming increasingly able to do sustained intellectual work with independence and enjoyment.

To say this much is already to foreshadow many questions and tensions: the different roles of faculty and student in a common enterprise, authority and freedom, the relation between the common task and individual differences in interest and bent. We were quite radical in abandoning the normal lower-division structure. But we were not anarchic, or individualistic, or student-interest-oriented. We had a common, completely "required" curriculum.

A common required curriculum is not, in fact, incompatible with the useful and necessary recognition of individual differences. But the common program may need to be protected and the legitimacy of its overriding demands acknowledged. We had indicated, in general terms, what the program would involve so that students who chose to enter were aware of what they were committing themselves to. Beyond that, we planned to keep the common core to dimensions which would leave time for the pursuit of related special interests; and we provided for a wide range of choice in term projects and even in the regular papers. It seems quite possible to provide adequate scope for differences while developing a common core.

If we stress the significance of the common core it is because we wish to make it clear that in avoiding the Charybdis of courses, subjects, and classes we do not seek refuge in the Scylla of "what the student is interested in." There are programs and institutions based on that principle, but ours is not one of them.

III

The First Year

We asked the students, when we notified them early in August of admission to the program, to read Herodotus before the semester began. We spent the initial three weeks of the semester on the *Iliad* and then a two-week period on the *Odyssey*, Xenophon's *Anabasis*, and Hesiod's *Works and Days*. Against this background we spent three weeks on Thucydides' *History*, supplemented by some of Plutarch's *Lives* and some Aristophanes; then a week on the *Oresteia* of Aeschylus, a week on the Theban trilogy of Sophocles, and a three-week period on Plato's *Republic*, *Apology*, and *Crito*. This brought us to the Christmas break. We suspended our normal operation for the rest of the semester, asking the student to devote the two weeks of vacation and the three following weeks to relatively independent work on a project of special interest related to what we had all been studying. Five papers were assigned during the semester and, in addition, many students wrote longer papers in connection with their term projects, although a paper was not required.

The second semester began with a seventeenth-century best seller, the Bible (King James Version), on which we spent about four weeks. This was followed by about four weeks on Shakespeare: essentially the historical plays and *King Lear*, about four weeks on Hobbes' *Leviathan*, and a final three weeks on Milton's *Paradise Lost*. We also asked the student to read a history of seventeenth-century England as, for example, Trevelyan's *History of England under the Stuarts*. There was also a term project on which the student was to be working during the entire semester. We assigned only four papers during this semester but expected more writing in connection with the term project.

This was the general pattern. Some comments follow.

The Readings

The readings defined the work of the program in the sense that, at any particular time the answer to "What are we doing?" was: "We are reading————."

We had to guard against the tendency to add to the basic list. We preferred a few good things handled in depth to many good things read in haste. Keeping the core small permitted intensive reading and rereading. It also gave students time to do additional reading on their own initiative in related primary or secondary materials. We felt that, generally, students are required to read so much that they can hardly read at all, or can hardly read with a sense of leisure and enjoyment.

We also preferred primary to secondary material. We wanted to read the *Iliad* rather than what scholars and critics said about the *Iliad*; or, at least, we wanted to read the *Iliad* first.

Obviously, we read the Greeks in translation. We apologize to everyone. But it was either the Greeks in translation or no Greeks at all. We regret that they chose to write in Greek, but we do not regret reading something like them in English.

It should be noted that "three weeks" on the *Republic* or on Thucydides—since that is, except for one outside course, the student's only assignment—amounts to almost a full semester three-unit course in terms of time. It is, of course, concentrated, but it provides a qualitatively unique and significant experience.

Clearly, the readings develop persistent and recurring themes. We did not, however, attempt to organize the reading about these themes—moving, let us say, from a speech in Thucydides to a section of *Antigone* to the *Crito* to develop a view about "law." We read each work as a whole, generally in temporal order. It required less orchestration.

On the whole, the reading list was the most successful feature of the program. The faculty felt increasingly justified in the selections, and the students, while responding differently to different works, found the reading rewarding and exciting.

The major challenge of the reading was, of course, to learn to read; that is, to learn to read slowly and thoughtfully, to savor the quality of character and situation, to ask fruitful questions, to follow and assess arguments, and to enjoy the process. Preoccupation with rapid reading, overlong assignments, and graded examinations have gone a long way toward destroying the art. Academic reading has become, for many students, not a mental activity but a physical ordeal. This is a real scandal.

Term Projects

Each semester, in addition to the common reading and its related writing, we provided for a special or term project. The first semester, as has been mentioned, we concluded the common reading program before the Christmas vacation and asked the students to devote the vacation and the three weeks after vacation to work on a special project. We asked that they pursue in depth some aspect of Greek life or culture that seemed to them especially interesting and significant. Thus, they might spend the five weeks reading Greek tragedy and get into secondary and critical literature; or they could study Greek politics, religion, history, or art. This, we thought, would give them a chance to pursue individual interests related to the common program.

We originally spoke rather loosely of a "term paper" and it soon became clear that the problem of producing a paper—and a term paper at that—was taking some of the joy out of life and drastically modifying the shaping of the work. Since, at this point, we were more interested in having the student roam and explore we made it clear that writing a paper was optional and that we would accept a brief description of the work or reading done if the student did not write a paper.

Many of the students did a great deal of interesting work during this period, and some good papers were turned in. On the whole this break in the routine was welcome to all and the time was well spent.

During the second semester we attempted a different sort of project. Without a Herodotus and a Thucydides, the history of the first half of the seventeenth century in England did not receive much direct attention. And while we asked the students to read Aubrey's *Lives* and a standard history of the period, we thought that something more was needed. The core readings —the Bible, Shakespeare, Hobbes, and Milton—were fairly cosmic in setting, and we wanted something that would, in contrast, provide an immersion in the concrete complexities of the situation. We hit on the following device: each student was to select a person whose life was significantly involved in the characteristic crises of the period; as, for example, Cromwell or Charles or Laud, or Wentworth, or Milton, and was to take this person as a secondary focus for the entire semester. The student was to attempt, through essentially biographical study, to understand him, his problems, his decisions. We thought that in this way the student would be getting an interesing grasp of the history of the period. Again, the writing was optional. But we suggested that the students might organize a Cromwell circle or a Milton circle, etc., to pursue the common interest together.

It was, we think, a very good idea. But nothing much happened. The circles never formed and many students never really got started. Some students picked topics which were not really in the spirit of the assignment. It should also be said that some students worked vary hard and profitably at the project and are even continuing work during the summer.

Both projects were, we think, good ideas. But the second semester's project was clearly a victim of underorganization.

Writing

We assumed from the very beginning that writing was an important part of the program, and we expected to assign a paper every two or three weeks. This represented less a judgment about the proper amount than the conviction that the student should be steadily under the necessity of bringing his work to careful expression. Writing is, of course, an art; but we thought of it as a useful pedagogic tool, as revealing the student's mind and as providing a basis for helpful analysis and criticism. A copy of each paper is kept on file so that we have available for reference all of the student's written work.

We drifted into asking for less than we had expected to, since the writing assignments tended to coincide with reading blocs. Thus, if we were on the Bible for a month we asked for one paper on the Bible. We ended up with nine or ten papers on average, although some students wrote more. On the whole, students turned in their papers promptly, although, of course, some did not. Again, on the whole, the assignment was taken seriously, although many papers were obviously done in a superficial, hasty, and perfunctory manner. Length varied, some students averaging 4-5 pages, others 10-15 pages. The range in quality was from unusually good to very poor. But we are in no position as yet to hazard a judgment about the general quality of performance and what it may reveal about the nature of the program.

The student's work needs prompt and careful analysis and criticism. This imposes a considerable burden on the faculty, and our response may, in many respects, have been inadequate. Usually the professors read half the papers, and the teaching assistants read half. We were, in principle, to pay attention to everything: spelling, sentence structure, organization, coherence, clarity, ideas. In practice, correction, comment, and criticism varied considerably with the reader. Some of us were more practiced, with a better eye for detail, and more patience, than others. Some jumped hard on what others passed over lightly. Since the student is assigned to a different professor each semester he should come eventually under a wide range of critical scrutiny.

Written criticism was supplemented in many cases by discussion in conference, although we could not have a conference with each student on each paper.

We still have much to learn about the form in which writing assignments should be made. Should we simply say, "Write a paper on Thucydides?" Or should we say something specific and directed: "Write a speech in which you take part in the debate about Mytilene." How much choice should the student have, etc.?

Behind such questions lurks an interesting controversy about writing as "expression," as an exercise in "creativity," as something done freely and spontaneously, and writing as an exercise to be done willy-nilly, as, at worst, a "task" to be performed at a certain time and in a certain way because it is judged, by a teacher, to be an educationally useful activity. The faculty was not of one mind on this question; nor were the students. It is a fundamental problem, or at least an aspect of a fundamental problem. Everyone seems to be for "freedom"; but is freedom to be understood in terms of mastery and discipline or in terms of impulse, inclination, and release—that is the question. At any rate, some cosmic questions come to bear on the assigning of student writing, and we will surely have the answer before the end of the year.

Individual Conference

We have said that, in accepting a 30-1 ratio we were, in principle, accepting an arrangement which precluded systematic use of the "individual tutorial" method of instruction. Some private institutions with ratios of 6-1 through 10 or 12-1 can, if they wish, make the individual tutorial the rock upon which they build. But quite apart from the question of its merit—and it is a real question—it is not an option for the typical institution in the modern world. The individual conference can be invaluable. It is also very demanding and exhausting. We could not, and did not attempt to, meet all our students regularly in private tutorial session.

The trick is to keep faculty time sufficiently free so that when a student needs a conference he can have one. And this may be a session of several hours during which the student's work and his problems can be explored in helpful depth. Sometimes a student will be aware of his need for a conference; sometimes the faculty member must take the initiative as he becomes aware of the need when he reads a student paper, or hears the student in section, or perhaps notices his absence. The problem, then, has two aspects: providing time, and sensing when a conference is needed.

Our involvement in conference varied widely. One professor, at least, tried to see most of his students about most of the papers and was clearly overworked. Some of us may not have been sufficiently available.

The individual conference can be of such crucial importance that, of course, we must have it. But, if it is done as it should be, its demands are heavy. It hardly needs to be said that the conference, however academic the initial focus, inevitably makes the faculty member aware of a frightening range of problems, most of which he is not professionally prepared to face and all of which have a bearing on the student's education. It should also be said that conferences can be utterly delightful.

The Seminar

We planned, initially, that each student would attend one seminar each week in a group of fifteen. It was also expected that on Tuesday, if there was no afternoon program, or even as part of the afternoon program, we would meet in groups of thirty for an hour. We had not planned that teaching assistants would conduct sections or seminars on a regular basis.

Our practice drifted in several directions. The meetings of thirty were generally found unsatisfactory, and some professors split the group with the teaching assistant. In some cases the professor would also divide the seminar of fifteen into two groups. Each professor handled the seminar situation as he thought best. In the general press of work the staff devoted relatively little time to discussion of this phase of the work, so that differences remain largely unanalyzed.

That the seminar had a place in the program we took for granted. It is a standard teaching institution, and fifteen seemed, abstractly, an ideal number. We thought of it as a discussion session, but what that is, or should be, is not always clear.

The focus for discussion was obviously to be the material we were reading. But the instructor was presented with the usual range of alternatives, including talking too much himself. Should he pose the question for the day and insist on relevance and development? Or should he throw open the door to whatever anyone wanted to bring in or up? Should he insist on universal participation, call on silent students, ration the articulate, or should he let the reins go? And so on.

Some sessions were very stimulating, and some were frustrating and disappointing. Wide open discussion seemed to some to "go nowhere"; directed discussion might go somewhere but, as likely as not, to the wrong place. There was some desire expressed for more section meetings, but the demands on faculty time were already too great. There appears to be general agreement that fifteen is, in fact, not a very good number, and we have some variations in mind for next year.

Lectures

The Tuesday lecture occupies a place of special importance in the program. It is the only occasion on which we are all formally together, so that it is a college or program "assembly" as well as an academic exercise. Its potential influence on the tone or spirit of the whole enterprise—for good or for ill—is very great. We knew this and, from beginning to end, worried a great deal about Tuesday. It was, perhaps, the staff's greatest failure.

We expected the common Tuesday program to develop and reinforce a sense of unity and of involvement in a common enterprise. It is encouraging, occasionally, to see the idea in the flesh. But apart from ritual and ceremonial value, it provides an opportunity for the student to hear from professors other than the one to whom he is assigned for the semester, to be presented with a range of views and attitudes.

Our conception of the "lecture" itself was that it was primarily to sharpen and clarify the issues and problems developed by, or implicit in, the materials we were reading. We expected that there would be much disagreement and controversy which, openly expressed, would spark the program—driving us all more deeply into the material, more eagerly into discussion and argument.

It was clear, however, that we were letting ourselves in for something radically different from the normal university lecture. Usually when we lecture, we lecture on a subject in a field in which we have some professional competence, or at least an academic degree. That, of course, was not our situation. Professional competence in what was before the house was accidental or coincidental. We were drawn from literature, law, political science, mathematics, and philosophy; but we were not in the program as representing our special fields, and we were not, at this point, to fall lamely and belatedly back on ourselves and lecture on our respective specialties. Nor were we, in an amateur way, to bone up desperately on different subjects in order to give lectures which are given regularly and better in departmental courses. We were to be studying what the students were studying, and, as old hands, we were to take the lead in sharpening the issues.

The fact is, we suffered a general failure of nerve and, with some exceptions, the Tuesdays fell apart and dwindled, to revive sporadically when deliciously real faculty quarrels boiled over into public view.

Apart from the "professional competence" question a chief difficulty seems to be that we are not, in our teaching, accustomed to working with each other or even in each other's presence. An occasional irresponsible visitor is one thing, an active critical colleague is quite another; the visitor politely watches you mislead *your* students, the colleague observes with consternation that you are ruining *his*.

Vanity (more charitably, insecurity) also enters the picture. Each of us develops his own style as he adjusts to the demands of the classroom. Some deliver carefully prepared and polished lectures, some work from detailed outlines and notes, some seem to make things up as they go along. We are not reluctant to sparkle, but we don't sparkle in the same way or in the same setting. Thus, every proposal—that we do this or that next Tuesday—was likely to be uncongenial to some of us. We recognized this, drifted into a system of reluctant volunteering, and were so grateful for anyone's efforts that we were hesitant to take issue or criticize.

At any rate, the Tuesday lectures by the staff were sometimes interesting and stimulating and sometimes not. The quantity tended to fall off, and we had fewer "full" Tuesdays than we had expected. The staff was generally dissatisfied and worried about the problem, and the students frequently were disappointed.

The lecture program as a whole was greatly helped by the generous response of the Berkeley faculty to invitations to speak. We had about a dozen guest lecturers during the year, invited to speak about subject in their fields as these were relevant to the work of the program. These lectures were much appreciated by students and staff. Our usual practice was to invite an outside speaker only after we had a chance to study the material, and under these circumstances the lectures were eagerly anticipated. They gave us a refreshing glimpse of the professional at work. Requests by students for "more lectures like that" usually followed, and many students undertook, more or less systematically, to audit lecture courses outside the program.

A good deal of thought will have to go into the improving of this important feature of the Experimental Program.

The House

A physical center is essential to the program. An obvious and traditional possibility is to take over a dormitory, converting some space to office and academic use. In our search for a center we considered this possibility briefly. Space is scarce, and there is some dissatisfaction with the present structure of dormitory life, so that some form of residential lower-division college within the larger university community merits further consideration. But it was not clear that we could make the necessary arrangements in time, and, in any case, we were reluctant to take on an additional set of problems.

Our needs were, we thought, adequately provided for when we were assigned the use of an old, recently vacated fraternity house at the north edge of the campus. Something needs to be said about the physical situation since it is not without its effect on the spirit.

We had the use of two floors. Faculty offices took up the top floor. The main floor provided a large, wood-paneled, befireplaced commons room or lounge, a large library or reading room, several small lounges or conference rooms, the secretary's office, and, in the old kitchen, a coffee-making machine. The offices were furnished with standard office furniture. The reading room had two long library tables with chairs for thirty or forty. There were several hundred paper-backs on the shelves, mostly contributed by publishers. Apart from a variety of collapsible or portable chairs and some tables we had virtually no furniture. A special grant of $1000 provided a large, badly needed rug for the commons room and a hi-fi set. The Law School contributed two old sofas. The mother of one of our students sent us several dozen attractive cushions. And that was it.

The result was a combination of charm and ugliness. Visitors, charmed by the exterior, were appalled by the interior. It was probably no one's special fault, but the University's provision for the suitable furnishing of the center for its experimental program was simply a joke. And the effect of this on the use of the house is difficult to judge. Some students found the situation very attractive and even expressive of their metaphysical views about the universe and its furniture. Others simply found it unattractive and stayed away.

We expected that the house would be a beehive of activity: students eager to discuss the readings with each other and with stray faculty members, informal, ad hoc seminars, sessions with visitors, evening programs, etc., etc. We hoped that our students would generally hang out there and that the common intellectual interest would develop and flourish so that the formal seminars would only be interruptions in a continuous discourse.

Alas! These expectations were, no doubt, unrealistic. Berkeley is, for new students at least, a three-ring circus. The north edge of the campus is not where the action is, and students generally live on the south side. But whatever the contributing physical factors the explanation must be deeper. The use of the house was uneven and sporadic. For a small but active group the house

was almost home; for others it was strange and even hostile ter-
ritory; for most it was just there—sometimes visited, sometimes
not.

For the faculty, hearing their footsteps echo in a deserted
house could be a disconcerting experience. What have we done
wrong? Is the program dead? And things would seem dead for
a stretch of days, only to revive suddenly for no very clear
reason. The house was visible—with its flaws and disorder, its
dominant in-group, its absent throngs. Its condition was always
a sign of something, but a sign not easy to interpret.

IV

The special quality of the program is not adequately communi-
cated by this sketch of its formal and informal structure and
practice. The first year was marked by rapidly fluctuating moods
of exaltation and despair, of eagerness and weariness, of disillusionment and renewal of faith. It was a year of tension. It
is difficult to say how much was due to the special problems
of getting started, of breaking new ground, and how much is
built into the program. But this report would be seriously incomplete without some hint of the stresses and strains.

A group of students and faculty set out, in the midst of a
powerful, ongoing, somewhat turbulent institution, to develop
and engage in a radically different mode of educational life. We
were doing not only what we had not been doing before but
what others around us were not doing. And we were a more
or less conventional group of faculty members and a fairly
representative group of Berkeley freshmen.

We quickly came to realize how much shelter the normal
classroom situation provides for the professor. He sees his
class TuTh or MWF for an hour. Students arrive, pause briefly,

and depart. The professor is clearly in charge. He is on his own ground, a plenary grade wielder, protected by tradition and "academic freedom" from external and even colleagial scrutiny. He is responsible for only a small fraction of the students' education and need not concern himself about what happens elsewhere or about what it all adds up to. He faces a collection of individuals who are generally strangers to each other and who have only the slightest transient identity as a "group." Only extremely good or extremely bad teaching can transform a class into a community capable of developing and asserting the power of its own peer-group culture. And the subject, defined in disciplinary terms, permits the formulation of issues or problems in ways appropriate to the special perspective of the discipline and the professor. The standard mood is academic.

In our program, however, the faculty was without its usual insulation. We were exposed to each other at the point of the exercise of the art of teaching. And we were in contact with students in a radically different way. We were aware that we were almost entirely responsible for the students' education. The core problems—war and peace, freedom and authority, order and chaos—were problems with which they were vitally concerned, and the stakes were not merely academic tokens and counters. Moreover, the students came to know each other and to develop something of a sense of themselves as a group with interests which called for expression and assertion.

Conflict was not unexpected; although it is somewhat surprising that there was so little conflict or tension between the program and the outside world and so much that was generated internally—between faculty members, between students, and between faculty and students. Our foreign relations were amicable, our domestic life troubled. It was all very healthy and interesting—"all passion spent"—but it would be impossible as well as inappropriate to detail our family quarrels to even a friendly world.

It is impossible for the Berkeley faculty to be unaware of the deep-seated disaffection of large numbers of students. Youthful rebellion or generational conflict is, of course, old stuff. But it is always a real problem, and we face it in an aggravated form and from a fairly vulnerable position. Education involves initiation into the ongoing enterprises of a culture. But initiation is not a blind or mindless process; things must make sense. And, not without cause, large numbers of intelligent, sensitive, moral young men and women have come to doubt the sanity and integrity of their elders. We ask them to commit themselves to our democratic procedures and institutions as the best way to serve the ideals of peace, justice, freedom, equality. They see these procedures leading us into the morass of brutal war with, at best, shaky moral credentials. They are not captivated by the sterile quality of consumer life offered by our affluence. They find, or think they find, the betrayal of all ideals by tired, old, conventional hypocrites. They are not ready to join us.

Education in the context of the program is directly relevant to these concerns. The path is not easy nor the outcome assured. But at least we are involved in the great battles of the age. It should come as no surprise that conventional political categories—liberal, radical, conservative, left or right—were altogether unimportant. The issues are deeper, posing a challenge to the very notion of civilization and "order" and even to the value of rationality, coherence, and clarity. In this situation even questions of how to read and write tend to become ideological or metaphysical.

There were several "confrontations" during the year. Some students felt that the student body should have a share in the shaping of the curriculum, and while there was some discussion of the curriculum, formally and informally, the faculty reserved the right and power of decision to itself. We have a required curriculum, and students who commit themselves to the program must accept the authority of the faculty to determine the course of study. We have neither an internal elective system nor student determination of the structure of the common program. Given the temper of the current student generation, this is inevitably a fighting point.

In the same "authoritarian" spirit the faculty rebuffed a student move to attend or sit in on regular faculty meetings. And, toward the end of the year, having decided not to renew teaching assistant appointments, the faculty held to this decision in spite of a student petition requesting that the teaching assistants be given the option of continuing in the program. There were bruises and hard feelings all around.

In spite of (because of?) everything, the program not only survived the pains and crises of the first year but managed to end the year in high spirits.

There is no simple answer to "how is the program doing?" It has been, in many important ways, an exciting, fruitful, and significant experience for both students and faculty. Our faith in the fundamental educational conception is strong and unshaken. In fact, the idea is so sound that it triumphs over shortcomings and failures in execution at any point and even at every point. Contrary to rumor, we are not about to fold. We will take the first class through its second year and hope to take on the second freshman class in the fall of 1967.

The crucial, overriding problem is that of the availability of faculty. It is an important part of the conception of the program that it be staffed by regular members of the faculty on leave from their departments for one or two years. We do not want a separate lower-division faculty set apart to teach in the program on a permanent basis—although it would be relatively easy to recruit a faculty of able mavericks eager to come to Berkeley for this purpose. This may be a dogma worth re-examining, but the reasons are obvious to anyone familiar with the structure of faculty life in a large university. However, we wish not only to avoid the negative aspects of a separate "teaching faculty" but to make a positive point of the value of allowing or encouraging faculty members to take part, now and then, in radically different teaching programs. While this creates problems of stability, it also ensures freshness and could prevent an enterprise which goes dead from prolonging its physical existence through the operation of vested interests.

When we consider that a dozen faculty members could keep the program going at its present scale, admitting a new class each year, the difficulties do not appear to be too great. But they may prove formidable. There is a great deal of teaching energy and imagination in the non-tenure ranks. However, the pressures for professional achievement and departmental service are so great at this stage that it is hazardous for non-tenure faculty to participate in the program. At tenure ranks half the faculty seems either to be on leave or to be going on leave the next year, and the quarter system may add complications. And there are research projects, books and articles with deadlines, graduate program demands, departmental teaching responsibilities which have to be considered by even that relatively small proportion of the faculty which is interested in novel educational ventures in general and this one in particular. It is hoped that this report will evoke expressions of interest in possible participation in the program. It is becoming clear that, for institutional as well as important pedagogic reasons, the greatest hope lies in interesting relatively senior professors in the possibilities of participation.

All other problems are minor and manageable. *Staffing* is the serious problem. If we can solve that we can continue the program on a trial basis until the University, in due course, assesses its work and determines its fate.

Appendix: A Technical Note on Academic Bookkeeping

At the end of two years the student enters the regular program of the College of Letters and Science as a junior. In semester terms the program carries 48 units of credit. A single outside course each semester would bring the total to sixty or over.

The program is considered as satisfying the social science and humanities breadth-requirements and the reading and composition requirement. Students who have not satisfied the foreign language requirement when admitted must take a language course as their outside course. Normally, the language requirement will be satisfied by the end of the first year. This leaves only the science requirement which can be satisfied during the upper-division years or through the outside course during the sophomore, or, in some cases, the freshman year. Thus, students in the program are not excused from normal requirements; what the program itself does not reasonably fulfill is satisfied by regular courses.

Preparation or prerequisites for the major poses some problems. It is hoped that the outside course during the second year and, in some cases, summer session work, will be sufficient, without asking that departments waive their usual prerequisites. We intend, however, to explore with some departments the degree to which the program will be regarded as providing some preparation for the major in lieu of some regularly recommended or required freshman or sophomore courses. Obviously, students who look forward to science careers or majors will not be able to take our program unless they are prepared to take an extra year.

It is recognized that the program does nothing in the way of integrating science with the social sciences and humanities. We leave the two-culture problem for wiser men to solve. In this respect, however, our students are neither better nor worse off than others.

Students who transfer out of the program before the two years are completed are given 12 units of credit for each semester's work.

In spite of some pressure, we have generally held, and will continue to hold, that a student may take only one course outside the program. Under the quarter system the point of this is even more obvious. One outside course provides a change of pace, maintains contact with the traditional course life, and helps in satisfying requirements. More than a single outside course would, we think, have subtle but significant and adverse effects on the whole conception of the program. Of course, auditing lectures and any other use of the resources of the University is encouraged. Our students should live a normal, varied, active student life.

After much uncertainty, the grade situation has been clarified. We did not—could not, since legislation was necessary—announce "pass–not pass" grading as a feature of the program. It quickly became apparent that adoption of such a system was highly desirable, and we deferred grading until legislative action by the Berkeley Division made adoption of the "pass–not pass" system possible. The student is given an option. He can indicate at the beginning of the semester, whether he wishes to be graded on the "pass–not pass" or on the conventional letter grade system. During the first year all but a handful chose "pass–not pass." We will be interested to see whether this changes.

There are problems connected with "pass–not pass." What about scholarships, prizes, honors? transfer to other institutions? admission to graduate and professional schools? draft board? employers? parents? Since we keep a file of each student's work and know him quite well we are able to write letters where that is acceptable. And we are quite willing, at the request of the student, to do so. But we do not yet know the full dimensions of the problem. We do not want to drift into a double grading system, "pass, but if pressed B." "Pass–not pass" may be coming into more general use, but it is not without complications.

We have been uncertain about what to do in a number of "marginal" cases. Our procedure is a great break from the student's normal high-school work pattern. We expected that there would be some difficulty in adjusting, and that in some cases a good deal of time would be required. Our inclination is to stay with a student, to ride out some storms, to wait and see (and hope), rather than to make life easier for ourselves by quickly dropping our problems or resorting to disciplinary grading techniques. Toward the end of the first semester, about 14 students indicated that they were transferring out—for a variety of reasons. No students (remaining or transferring) were given "not pass" for the first semester, and we were quite aware that reasonably strict grading standards were not being cooly applied. Students were aware, however, of our judgment of the quality of their work. During the second semester, some of the marginal performers improved and some did not. A number, aware that they were not working well, decided to transfer out and subject themselves to the more familiar discipline of the regular program. In some cases, we advised transferring; and a review of the work this summer may well lead to more advice of this kind and even to some involuntary transfers.

The whole problem of grades and discipline is troublesome,

and we are not yet clear about what to do. A premature resort to grades, or to expulsion, as a means of providing discipline and motivation can easily destroy the possibility of developing a different kind of—and a deeper—motivation. But abandoning the traditional prods and checks also poses problems. We will need to watch this situation closely.

Draft of Report on Program, January 1968

The American college is the setting for a crucial rite of passage. Parents see it as the place where they lose their children. The son or daughter who leaves, uncertainly, in September reappears briefly in December moving to the music of some strange pied piper, lost forever. To the student, it is a world of peers without parents, the threshold to the broader stage of fools. To the society, which creates and sustains it, the college is a mysterious institution into which turbulent generations of adolescents are fed and from which are to issue, each year, intelligent, appreciative adults ready to take their places among the guardians of civilization.

The teacher knows that the college is the most crucial of battlefields. It is not simply that it is a place of confrontations— youth and age, feeling and habit, impulse and discipline, innocence and experience. It is the place where the essential vitality of the society is tested, its capacity to claim and harness the energy and commitmnt of its youthful self. The society brings itself, in the college, to public trial. There, before a skeptical, and even hostile, jury it must state its case. It must recollect and clarify its purposes, aims, and values; it must justify, if it can, its current interpretations of these purposes; it must acknowledge its shortcomings, explain its difficulties, justify its procedures, and reveal opportunities for creative and constructive action. The college is the point at which society comes to self-consciousness.

It is forced to do so by its very nature. It is the great social initiatory institution. It must make sense of the enterprise to which society expects the younger generation to commit itself. Habit goes a long way, and sheer momentum can carry us over some rough spots. But, in the end, we need more. In a "free" society the commitments of membership must be rooted in understanding.

The capacity of the college to make sense of the society which sustains it is the ultimate test of social vitality. If we cannot pass that test, we are doomed more certainly than by mere physical devastation. We cannot survive the breaking of the generational succession. Society, in the college, is not simply battling for the souls of men, it is fighting for its life.

The American college has been described in many ways, not always, or even usually, in these terms. The society which sustains it expects some return, but usually in the form of heightened competence for the professions and the more complex careers. The student sees it as serving his private needs. The faculty tends to think of itself as pursuing and transmitting knowledge. All these purposes find some measure of expression in the college. But they obscure the most significant fact. The college has come, more than any other institution in our secular "pluralistic" society, to fill the gap left by the separation of church and state; it performs some of the functions of an established church. It is the institution of initiation and confirmation. It is our failure to see this which is responsible for so much of the futility of current college reform. It is a failure of perception, and it is also a failure of nerve.

The society which imposes this task upon the college does

not make the task an easy one. It sends to it sons and daughters already deeply disaffected and disillusioned. They take for granted a fairly high level of material affluence, but they are not grateful nor are they impressed by the quality of life it has brought to their parents. They are deeply troubled by the war and the race question and tend to see these as the characteristic expressions of a society that has betrayed its ideals. With youthful ruthlessness they see the gap between professed ideals and practice as evidence of hypocrisy and condemn impatiently attempts to "explain the complexities" as mere establishment rationalization, as a defense of the "status quo."

The teacher, in this situation, rediscovers, if he has forgotten, the tale of the two cities—the enduring and the temporary, the invisible and the visible. He must fall back upon a conception of the community as enduring through time, an organization of intentions that, at any particular moment in its history, are imperfectly or inadequately expressed in the shape of its external and visible institutions. The mystery of initiation is that it is the joining of the invisible city, the commitment to ideals and institutions, not the mere acceptance of current practice. In short, the student has seen through some myths; he must now be initiated into the mystery. This initiation is not only the basis for appreciation, loyalty, and commitment, it is also the precondition of genuine dissent. It provides the understanding without which "dissent" cannot rise above mere opposition.

The visible gap between our ideals and our practice makes the initiatory task extremely difficult. At the same time, the disarray of the visible world forces the college, to its profit, to develop its philosophical resources. In meeting the challenge the college, out of educational necessity, may reforge a coherent and intelligible theory of the state.

Nothing is more badly needed. We have been drifting thoughtlessly on the wreckage of a shallow commercial individualism. But what has seemed to serve the father can no longer serve the son. Every bad theory exacts its price, and we are paying now.

It is deeply fitting and ironic that the students whose behavior most disturbs the adult world come to the college equipped with a "philosophy" which is only to a slight degree a parody of that of their elders. It is not the newness of the ideas which shocks; it is their haunting familiarity. Ivan is being confronted with Smerdyakov. Shall we review the standard items?

"The only language they understand is power." Authority? Legitimacy? Nothing but power clothing its nakedness in rhetoric. Principles? Rights? Rhetoric, unless there are battalions of bodies. International law and morality? It comes down to power. Therefore, student power. Very perceptive; very orthodox.

"Trust feeling; distrust reason and the word." If you buy and sell the mind, your children will become misologists. If you turn radio and television over to commerce, don't complain about the suspension of belief. A healthy organism tries to protect itself; the assaulted mind will turn against the word.

"Anyone over thirty is either dead or can't be trusted." Who do they know over thirty? And how, in any case, expect the young to resist the impact of the vast cosmetic industry which has sold the cult of youth to rueful parents.

Drugs? The obvious and traditional response of a consumer civilization to the news, "The Kingdom of Heaven is within you."

"It's my life." An outrageously silly application of a primitive notion of property to something the claimant has neither created nor nurtured.

"Everyone should do what seems right to him." Apparently the ultimate moral principle, casually relegating law, politics, experience, authority, knowledge, humility, and all that, to the dustbin of history. Moral solepcism and self-righteous idiocy. We do not see, apparently, that this is the classic characterization of the state of war.

This is a short way with a short list. But it suggests the problem. Students do not learn these things in college; it is part of their baggage when they arrive. They did not make it up. It is their going-away present from the middle class.

The college must transform this state of mind—which at most can barely support a shallow and parasitic private life—into something capable of sustaining and developing the life of a democratic society. It is not an easy task. And it is not clear that the college has either the will or the capacity to succeed. But it is the last hope, and the battle must be joined there.

The college faculty, if it had a voice, would raise it in indignant and horrified protest at this description of its function. "We are not," it would say, "a church; we are not an institution for moral reclamation; we are not the spiritual arm of the political state. We are a secular institution of higher learning in a pluralistic society. We are not the priests of your invisible city. Moreover, this is a democracy, and democracy is based on individualism not on your kind of thought control and—yes— totalitarianism. And furthermore, who are you, or we, to judge, to presume to teach virtue, to impose values on others. No, thanks! We are independent scholars, not grand inquisitors; humble truth seekers, not soul savers." Objection for objection, the guilty uneasiness of society and the desperation of the disillusioned student are as nothing compared with the adamant self-assurance of the faculty.

If there is a reply it must begin, I think, with an insistence on the distinction between the idea of the university and the idea of the college.

The university *is* an organization of scientists and scholars engaged in research. Its concern is with knowledge. Its teaching is professional and technical, centered in the graduate school. So great is its attractive power that it has warped the college into its own orbit. The college of letters and science has become simply a part of the university, a holding company for a large number of university departments with administrative responsibility for undergraduate education. But it has lost the sense of any independent mission. It measures success in terms of students sent on to graduate school; it is content to be a preparatory school for the professions, academic and other.

The college has drifted into this condition because it has never understood, or taken seriously, the implications of democracy. First, that democracy imposes on everyone, in the name of dignity and freedom, a political vocation. And second, that this vocation demands a special education. But the American college turned its back on this opportunity; and its institutional structure and the character and bent of its faculty make it highly unlikely that it will seize it now.

One of the consequences is that the college is ludicrously unprepared for the crisis in which it now finds itself. Its intellectual guns are trained in the wrong direction. It expects the administration to cope with major student unrest as if it were chiefly a question of bad manners. It meets the charge of educational irrelevance with bland incomprehension. Faced with a major moral and intellectual crisis, it presents its kaleidoscopic array of courses in subjects leading, ultimately, to the Ph.D. It does not see that this form of salvation is, for the college, only another way of dropping out.

The renewal of the college can and must begin with its first two years—the so-called lower division. The student is relatively free from immediate vocational pressure, although his search for a significant role is intense. His expectations are high; he is ready to turn over a new leaf; and he has not yet been discouraged into academic apathy by the discovery that his "important" problems are extra-curricular. He is ready for education.

Moreover, the college is less confident about its handling of the lower division than about the rest of its life. The major program is still generally confined to the upper-division years, and it is recognized that the student's college education should consist of more than a major. But what that "more" should be is not so clear, and the college is open to suggestion. I suggest that we consider this question under the rubric, *The First-Program Problem*.

The program is the significant educational unit. Programs may be, and usually are, constructed out of courses. The course is a familiar unit for teaching purposes, but it would generally be recognized—and the quarter system has brought this point home—that a single course is a fragment, and that much of its significance depends on the context of courses and other modes of organized intellectual effort in which it is placed.

Graduate work—the third program—is a program of sustained study designed by the faculty as adequate preparation for teaching and research in a particular field or area. A Ph.D. program may involve courses, but it is defined in terms of the mastery of knowledge and techniques, tested in various ways, and is thought of as a more or less coherent program.

The upper-division major—the second program—while it may often be defined in terms of courses is, in principle, a more or less coherent plan of study designed to give the student some immersion in the basic concepts, the problems, the lore, the methods and techniques which characterize one of the great academic disciplines. It is supposed to be more than just a collection of courses in a department. It is, in intention, a coherent program.

The difficulty is with the largely non-existent first program. (We seem to cover the range from programs without courses through programs with courses to courses without programs.) Can we construct and maintain, largely within the framework of our existing resources, a suitable variety of coherent and appropriate first programs?

What we have now, instead, is a loose system of "requirements." These have a long history and reflect genuine educational considerations. But, I believe, there is general dissatisfaction with what they add up to or fail to add up to. They are conceived as guarding against premature specialization by insisting on "breadth," a minimal sampling of courses in various areas; as providing for the tools or skills a college graduate should have, e.g. the ability to write and knowledge of a foreign language. To these general requirements are added those which departments impose as prerequisites for the upper-division major, amounting, in some cases, to as much as half of the student's lower-division course work.

The result is that, for most students, undergraduate education involves a single program (the major), supplemented by a variety of fragmentary courses. The suggestion here is that we think of undergraduate education as involving two programs and attempt to reclaim the lower-division years for appropriate first programs. "Appropriate" means, at least (1) some measure of coherence and integration and (2) an organizing principle different from that upon which the second program, the departmental major, is based. It is also suggested that, for the sake of the integrity of the first program, departments be encouraged to claim a larger share of the student's time during the upper-division years, and, in exchange, minimize the lower-division prerequisites for majors.

We must expect, realistically, that for the immediate future at least, the course will continue to be the unit out of which most programs will be constructed. Two encouraging tendencies are discernible, however: the student course load appears to be moving from five to four or even three, so that his attention is less fragmented and distracted; and we are beginning to think of double and even triple courses as providing greater opportunity for real curricular planning.

We need now, as we try to clear the ground for significant first programs, to consider whether the time has not come to loosen further or even drop the general system of requirements which give us the illusion but not the substance of educational planning. What would happen if we dropped them? Students would still, in large numbers, pursue the study of languages, although many who now go through the motions would not. Students would still seek courses which offered them an opportunity to improve the clarity and coherence of their writing. Our general requirements are a substitute for a serious educational advising system. If we do not feel that we can safely drop the requirements and rely on advice, we should at least be prepared to waive the requirements where they interfere with an acceptable first program. We should also avoid adding to the requirements on an ad hoc basis.

But to clear the ground for the first program does not tell us what it should be. We need to apply creative educational energy to this problem to develop a number of reasonable programs. The essential point is that each should be powerful enough to give character to and to dominate the student's lower-division years and should be distinct from but complementary to the upper-division major. There are some traditional precedents: Western civilization, world civilization, integrated humanities and integrated social studies, American studies. Such "core courses" might well be expanded in scope and treated as "double

courses" and extended over as much as a two-year period. Foreign culture or area studies, heavily language-based, could be
developed. Or urban studies. The first program problem is not
unsolvable. It simply needs to be recognized as *the* problem, and
the ground needs to be cleared so as to encourage a variety
of solutions.

The Experimental Program

The Experimental Program, now in its third year, is a first program. Technically, it can be regarded as a triple "course" extend-
ing over two years. Except for a single outside course each
quarter, it constitutes the student's total program for his lower
division years. It is regarded as satisfying the reading and composition, social science and humanities, and American history and
institutions requirements. The outside course permits the student to satisfy the language requirement and either the science
requirement or some prerequisites for the upper-division major.
The program is limited to 150 entering freshmen selected
randomly from among applicants and is staffed by six full-time
faculty members. Almost all of the students avail themselves
of the pass–not pass option.

While the Program has been conceived from the beginning as
an integral whole, it is possible to distinguish two aspects: its
curriculum or "subject," and its pedagogic structure. Each is an
important part of the experiment, but it has always been considered possible that the general structure might commend itself
to some who would not approve of the particular curriculum and
who might wish to experiment with something like the same
form and a quite different curriculum. I therefore shall discuss
separately the curricular and structural aspects of the Program.

Curriculum

The curriculum—"what we study"—always has been the most difficult aspect of the program to explain. Not only difficult, but really, when explained, so controversial and subject to misunderstanding that there has been a tendency on our part to settle for accurate but superficial descriptions rather than to face the serious task of explanation. Thus, we have pointed to our list of readings—a list so powerful as to seem self-justifying or to support a number of justifications.

Or, falling back on the original source of inspiration—Alexander Meiklejohn's experimental college—we have described the program as a variation of the Athens-America curriculum, focusing on Greece, seventeenth-century England, and America. True enough, but the program is really not "historical" in its conception or orientation.

It is more revealing to say that the curriculum is "problem-oriented," using materials which are, to some extent, historically clustered. The problems, however, are fundamental and perennial—that is, as contemporary as they are historical. Against the background of war and conflict we see men struggling to achieve peace and freedom, attempting to supplant power by legitimate authority, to embody moral values in a legal order, to reconcile submission to authority and the claims of conscience and individual judgment, to curb passion with reason, to tame destructive pride, to make wisdom operative in human affairs.

That we begin with the Greeks and end with America only serves to give force to the conception of a human culture persisting as it develops different forms, enduring in various modes of expression. The underlying assumption is, therefore, that there is indeed a common set of fundamental problems and that liberal education is the process by which we become more perceptively and sensitively involved in them. That these problems are supremely urgent and relevant today is obvious, especially to anyone who is at all aware of the freshman state of mind crudely sketched earlier in this paper. I argued then that the function of the college, as distinct from the university, is to deal with that state of mind as part of the process of initiation into the life and work of society. The suggestion that the lower-division first program address itself to this task finds expression in the curriculum of the Experimental Program.

In Homer and Hesiod, Herodotus and Thucydides, Aeschylus and Sophocles, and in Plato we have a constellation of fresh and powerful minds grappling with central issues. To continue the argument in seventeenth-century England—with (yes!) the King James Bible, Shakespeare, Hobbes, and Milton—is to tap the other great stream in our living tradition and to set the stage for the American venture. The study of America presents great curricular challenges and difficulties, and we are planning revisions in the second year of the program. But we certainly will retain, as a central thread, the concern with the Constitution, politics, and law.

So much, then, for the "subject." I turn now to some of the curricular principles involved.

(1) *Everyone is to study the same materials.* This is a practical necessity, if there is to be a useful set of common lectures and seminars. But it is more than merely a practical necessity. It is a necessary condition for the development of a learning *community* with all of its sustaining qualities. A student who chooses to enter the program finds himself subject to a completely required curriculum for two years. It is, moreover, a curriculum determined entirely by the judgment of the faculty. We consider curriculum construction to be one of our central responsibilities, and we are not apologetic about the assertion of our

authority at this point. It is almost the main service we perform for our students.

This means that we are not impressed with current tendencies to allow or encourage each student to pursue his own "interests" or to encourage students collectively to participate in curriculum determination. Students will have the rest of their lives to plan their own learning programs; in college, such planning is still the responsibility of the faculty. As for motivation, students are interested in fundamental problems, and a program which deals with such problems intelligently will ellicit and sustain interest and effort. Moreover, the chief problem for the student is not interest but habit. Finally, a healthy student will be interested in what he should be interested in, whether he knows it or not. Our problem is to shape programs which embody what the student should be interested in. If we do that there will be no real problems of motivation.

(2) *The common reading list should be short.* Serious reading is almost a lost art. Rapid reading under pressure is killing it. It is essential to restore the activities of reflection, of questioning, of appreciation to the reading process. This takes time. Students must be given the chance to read at a more leisurely pace. This means staying with a relatively short list of readings, allowing sufficient time for each, and reading one thing at a time. For example, we spend three or four weeks on Plato's *Republic*. Since it is the only thing we read during that period, the time available is at least the equivalent of a major quarter course. Lectures, seminars, and papers during this period also are focused on the *Republic*. This adds up to an educationally unique experience, and the program is designed to provide an integrated sequence of such experiences—intense, but unhurried and undistracted.

The pace of the reading is always a difficult matter of judgment, but our situation is kept flexible so that the tentatively scheduled time for a particular work can be shortened or extended as we think desirable.

We are, of course, confronted with some difficult decisions and temptations. There are too many good things not on the list. We have Plato, but why not Aristotle? Why not more Euripedes? *Paradise Lost*, but why not Dante? The temptation is always to add good things, but we are convinced that that is the shortest path to disaster. No doubt it is possible to draw up a sequence of readings quite different from ours—perhaps equally good, perhaps better—although I doubt it. But it is not possible to draw up a list which would include every reasonable suggestion and still be an intelligible or manageable educational program. Choice is necessary, and it must be guided by considerations of thematic development, by concern for significance and variety, by a broad range of considerations that, for a teacher, are often intuitive; and experience will suggest modifications.

Our curriculum, then, takes as its "subject" a cluster of perennial moral and political problems and takes as its materials a relatively short and varied list of great works drawn from the Western tradition, to some extent historically clustered, and culminating in the study of these problems in the American context.

This particular curriculum is not an inherent or necessary part of the idea of a first program, and we can imagine a range of variations from those which keep the same central concerns but substitute other books for ours, to those which substitute major historical "clusters" including "non-Western" materials, to those which would depart radically from the central moral and political themes.

But a common, required, faculty-determined curriculum is an essential part of this conception of a first program.

Structure

The program makes a radical break with the course-classroom-examination pattern of educational life. But the problem is not simply to free the student from the traditional routine and turn him loose. It is, rather, to establish a ritual which will support and encourage the development of a set of intellectual habits consistent with a reasonable, effective, and continuous use of the mind. The association between "taking courses" and "getting an education" needs to be broken. But something must be put in the place of the old destructive routine. Just as we regard the development of the curriculum as a faculty responsibility, so also we regard the establishment and maintenance of a structure of educational occasions, activities, and demands as a faculty responsibility. The teaching art at this point is the art of maintaining an environment and ritual conducive to the development of intellectual powers and habit. The chief resource available, apart from the curriculum itself, is teaching judgment and energy, and the problem is to determine the structure of its most fruitful application.

The program makes use, in its own way, of the traditional techniques and forms: lectures, discussion, writing, conference.

Lectures. While we do not regard lecturing as the chief mode of teaching, it does have a significant place in the program. The dangers are familiar and obvious. The lecture can shift the work from the student to the teacher and encourage passivity; it can explain what the student should be trying to figure out himself; it encourages the confusion of "telling" with "teaching;" it presents the teacher with temptations. Nevertheless, meetings with a large number of students during which the faculty is being heard can, if properly conceived, be very useful. We have two such regularly scheduled meetings (each about 1½ hours long) a week, and all students and all faculty members are expected to attend.

The lecture program is coordinated with the readings, and its main function is to stimulate and deepen the reading process. We operate with a few simple rules. We do not lecture about what has not been read; and we do not generally present background or supplementary information. We try, instead, to raise questions, to offer suggestive interpretations, and to sharpen and deepen the issues or problems latent in the reading.

We have tried a variety of forms: occasionally a single speaker lecturing for almost the standard hour; sometimes two speakers for shorter periods; sometimes even three. We have had a few panel discussions. There is almost always a question or discussion period, with the faculty, on this occasion, given priority. Students have a chance to hear the views of the entire faculty, and while we do not strive artificially for controversy, it takes place quite naturally.

The common lecture program is quite indispensable. It is the only occasion on which we are all assembled. It ensures that common themes are developed and it reinforces the unity of the program. It keeps the faculty working closely together and gives the student a sense of involvement with more than members of his own seminar group. As the function of the lectures has become clearer the pressure on the faculty has virtually disappeared. We are not, except accidentally, academic experts on the material studied, and any attempt to give conventional academic lectures would be misguided. But we are not using the materials in the usual academic way in any case, and the faculty quite easily can develop, with the aid of a good deal of free internal criticism, the capacity to respond fruitfully to the materials. There is scope for a wide variety of approaches and styles. In short, the lecture program has become an interesting challenge to the faculty and a stimulating and unifying feature of the program.

Seminars. The seminar is the occasion for discussion, in a small group, of the curricular materials and ideas. We began with a single two-hour meeting each week with fifteen students. This was found to be unsatisfactory because fifteen seemed to be too large a group, and because one meeting a week did not seem to be enough. We then tried groups of about eight, each group meeting twice a week—once with the faculty member present and once without. This was much better, although it quickly became apparent that the second meeting, unattended by the faculty member, needed more attention. We are now going to try groups of ten or eleven, with increasing concern for the second meeting. The complexity of the seminar situation is so great that, for example, the faculty spent hours considering the advisability of the shift from eight to ten.

The question of appropriate size is, of course, related to the conception of the function of the seminar—more particularly to the role of the faculty member. If he is, in effect, to lecture there is not much point to smallness. If he is to dominate and direct the discussion to themes or ideas he believes to be most significant he may well be able to work with a larger group. If students are to be encouraged to discuss *with each other*, a small group is desirable and the discussion may move in directions the faculty member may not think most fruitful; and, in any case, his participation takes on a different character. A dominant role for the faculty, member means that the two seminar meetings are radically different in character. Should the objective be to foster the art of discussion so that the faculty member's presence becomes increasingly unimportant and the two meetings come to resemble each other in character? These are fascinating pedagogic questions, and the staff is not fully in agreement about them. There is general agreement, however, that the seminars are to focus on the current reading.

The regularly scheduled seminar without a faculty member present seems to us to be a promising institution adaptable to situations other than ours. It puts burdens and responsibilities squarely upon the students, and they are often surprised by the discovery of the extent to which they are, disappointingly, faculty-dependent.

Writing. The program makes it possible to think of student writing as a central educational discipline sustained over a two-year period. While there is some difference of opinion on this point, we do not, on the whole, think of turning students into "writers." We are more concerned with the practice of writing as an activity which reveals the mind at work and aids in the development of clarity, coherence, and understanding. Whatever else it may be, writing is, for us, a powerful pedagogic instrument.

We expect, or hope, that the student will spend at least an hour a day writing—every day for two years. We assign a formal paper about once every two weeks. And we ask the student to write every day in his journal. This is not a personal diary. The student is to develop some idea growing out of the reading, discussion, or lecture, and the journal is to be available for faculty scrutiny.

We are moving with increasing conviction toward formal papers on clearly assigned topics and in a prescribed form. And we are discovering that we have much to learn about how to formulate paper assignments so as to increase the possibility that the writing will be educationally productive.

In the past, we have returned the papers with written comments and corrections (keeping a copy for the student's file) and on occasion have discussed the paper with the student in individual conference. But we are not too pleased with this method. Paper reading is a lot of work, and written comments are not always helpful or effective. We are now going to try regular tutorial conferences. We plan to see each student once every two weeks for a half hour, during which we will read and discuss the paper with the student. We hope this will provide for an effective level of attention, analysis, and criticism. The provision for this regular individual conference is related to our decision to increase the size of the seminar to ten students.

The writing program heightens our awareness of the problems of habit. Our students, for example, have coped effectively with high school demands. The standard habit is deadline-oriented: reading delayed until late, a writing strategy adopted, a last-minute sustained writing session, a marginal revision while typing. It is difficult and necessary to break this pattern and to develop another. The crucial experience is probably that of the student's own ruthless criticism of his first draft and the re-thinking involved in writing the second draft. But this requires *early* reading and thinking and an early writing of the first draft. Everyone knows this should be done, but it is easier said than done. Similarly, everyone agrees that the daily journal writing is a good idea. But apparently it is very difficult to find an hour each day, to sit down and try to write. It takes character and discipline.

Individual conferences. We have always assumed that our faculty-student ratio precluded regular tutorial sessions with each student. Our policy has been to consult individually with students whenever "needed." This has, indeed, worked fairly well, although it is possible and inevitable that a student who needs a conference may go unnoticed. Our decision to handle the formal papers on a conference basis will alter this situation. We will see every student once every two weeks. If this proves

to be an adequate way to criticize the writing, we will have
gained tutorial advantages as well.

Informal associations. From the beginning we have regarded
a physical "center" as essential to the program. We have relatively few formal "classes" or meetings, and we count on informal association and contact to strengthen the sense of the
common enterprise and community. A reconverted fraternity
house on the edge of the campus has been assigned to our
exclusive use and has been adequate for our needs. It is near
the auditorium which we use for the lecture program and, except for the lectures, all our academic activities take place in the
house. Keys are given to students on request and the house is
available for use evenings and weekends.

It is hard for us to think of the program without the house.
But it must be admitted that the house has been and continues
to be a source of disappointment and anxiety as well as of en-
lightenment.

Two Passing Observations

(1) This description has stressed the fact that both the curriculum and the structure are faculty determined, and that the program is, internally, "required." This obviously raises questions
about "freedom" and "authority" in education at the college
level, and the program may seem reactionary and authoritarian
in spirit. That is, it may seem so to those who understand neither
freedom nor education. I mention this point only to indicate
that I am perfectly aware of this misconception. Freedom is the
essence of the program.

(2) In this account of the Experimental Program as a "first
program," I have distinguished the "curriculum" from the
"structure" and have suggested that the conception of our cur-

riculum is not necessarily built into the broader idea of the first program. And in an obvious sense, this is the case. A different curriculum could be adopted. But I would be less than candid if I did not express my intolerant conviction that our curriculum comes close to being essential to the conception of a significant first program. I do not mean that this or that particular book is essential; or even that different historical clusters might not be used. But rather that the curriculum must be concerned with central moral, political, or social problems, that it must be concerned with initiation into the great political vocation.

I have little expectation that this view will be widely accepted. However, I believe that the first program, even apart from the curricular question, is a neutral and useful conception. It sharpens and clarifies some aspects of the question of how to handle the lower division.

The Problem of Institutionalization

The institutional fate of the Experimental Program is still to be determined. There are two questions. First, does the Program, as a mode of educational life, commend itself to the University as a reasonable and acceptable form of lower-division education? And second, can the University provide for its continuity and continuing vitality?

Evaluation is difficult. The traditional lower-division "programs," if they can be called that, are not really evaluated. Individual courses generally are sponsored by departments and approved by faculty committees, but beyond that there is little "evaluation." We rest on tradition and ad hoc judgment. The Experimental Program, as a drastic departure from standard practice, will seem to need special justification, but it is difficult to see what that would be.

Of the 150 students who entered the first class, ninety completed the program. Roughly, twenty students left the program at the end of each semester. Most transferred into the regular program, some left school for a variety of personal reasons. Of the ninety who completed the program, about fifteen are taking a junior year abroad or elsewhere, a few have dropped out for a while, and the rest are continuing at Berkeley. It will be some time before we even know how they fare in their upper-division programs, and it is not clear what that will prove.

We are skeptical about evaluation procedures and reluctant to get heavily involved in them. We recognize, however, that if the program is to continue it must receive faculty sanction beyond the authorization sufficient for its experimental phase. A case for the program will have to be made, but apart from giving its rationale and reporting the experience, we do not really know what to do or what will be required.

Moreover, the problems of continuity or institutionalization are so complex that, unless we can see the way to their solution, there is not much point in worrying about evaluation.

The chief problem is staffing. The difficulty of first-program staffing in an institution like the University at Berkeley, especially a first program like the Experimental Program, is so great that it is tempting to abandon the task as more fitting for institutions with a primary commitment to undergraduate education. But Berkeley does have a lower division, and what it does with it can have a significant effect on the freedom of other institutions to experiment with first programs. It should and must exercise some leadership in this field. Unless it loosens up, other institutions, confronted with the transfer problem, are unable to do so.

The heart of the matter is that a university faculty does not take naturally to college first-program teaching which is not "disciplinary." It can provide excellent lower-division courses which are introductory to majors, but it has great difficulty in doing anything else. All of the pressures, personal as well as institutional, drive the faculty into research and the research-related teaching which is the primary function of the university. The kind of lower-division teaching we tend to have is the kind which can be done without drastic or sustained diversion from research. The alternatives seem to be either to recruit a separate or special "college faculty" or to take more advantage than we now do of the different phases in the career of the faculty member. He is not always in a "technical" phase, and there are times when a different kind of teaching would be refreshing rather than distracting.

The separate college faculty problem is an old one, and no one is very eager to follow that path; certainly, not on a large scale. But it does not seem unreasonable to consider a small number of permanent appointments of men of high intellectual quality and training who are good at and committed to under-graduate teaching, and who would provide leadership and energy.

The Experimental Program has found six faculty members and our initial group of 150 students a satisfactory arrangement. A single faculty member permanently assigned to the program probably could handle the recruiting and orienting of the temporary staff (one or two years) and provide direction for the program, although a core-staff of two would be much better. A half-dozen permanent appointments would keep the program going at its present scale with a class beginning every year. The non-permanent staff would be recruited from the regular Berkeley faculty or from other institutions.

But "permanent" needs some qualification. A tenure appointment would be necessary. But we do not know how long one could take the strains of this form of teaching; or how long one would stay fresh. So we are back to joint appointments with alternative academic status and function where necessary or desirable.

The difficulties stressed here are those related to establishing and maintaining a non-disciplinary first program in a university setting. Many of the difficulties are diminished in colleges which do not think of themselves as universities. And, in universities, they become less formidable to the degree that first programs are conceived which draw more directly on the normal disciplinary competence of the faculty. But the danger to the university-dependent first programs is precisely at that point. The application of the disciplinary competence to the first program can easily mean an earlier professionalism barely mitigated by familiar pieties and clichés.

For lovers of knowledge, worshiping the sun, real lower-division first program teaching is the descent into the cave.

Postscript, July 1968

I. *Tutorials*

Our initial view was that our student-faculty ratio precluded regular individual tutorials, that we were to be available for conferences "as needed." This meant a fairly heavy, though irregular, conference schedule, usually focused on student papers; but no attempt was made to see everyone routinely. In the winter quarter of 1968 we shifted to regular individual tutorial sessions and, after two quarters' experience, regard them as an economical and essential feature of the program.

We introduced the system when attrition had reduced the student-faculty ratio to 20-1. We proposed to meet each student once in every two-week period—ten tutorial conferences each week. We planned on 30-45 minutes for each conference, although in practice it often ran longer.

The tutorial was devoted, for the most part, to analysis of the student's written work. We had found—what I suppose everyone finds—that taking a batch of student papers home, reading them, correcting mistakes, and writing comments intended to be diagnostic and helpful is among the more depressing and futile of academic exercises. A conscientious paper reader may spend an hour reading and marking up a five-page student paper, and the student may spend five minutes looking at the comments with very little profit.

It is an altogether different situation when the student and professor, each with a copy of the student's last written effort, settle down to consider it. The professor is reading it for the first time, questioning and commenting as he does so; the student is responding and explaining and often is giving his own paper its first objective reading. A characteristic mode of expression or error can be discussed until the point is grasped. And the discussion can cover a range of related questions.

The importance of such a conference needs no laboring. What is very worth noting, however, is our discovery that it adds up to a saving in faculty time. The instructor does no paper reading outside the conference session. And the regularly scheduled conference serves in lieu of a schedule of general office hours and obviates most of the need for special conferences. Faculty time is valuable, and eight hours a week is about the limit of time available for individual tutorials. This requires a rather severe limit to about 30 minutes when the ratio is around 25-1. An extra 15 minutes makes a significant difference, and as students, inevitably, drop out, it becomes possible to extend the time of each conference. Even a relatively short conference, however, is extremely valuable, and we are very happy about the way the tutorial has worked out.

II. *Teaching Assistants*

In view of the practice of making heavy use of graduate students as teaching assistants in lower-division courses, something should be said about our unwillingness to employ them in the program.

In our first year the staff consisted of five regular faculty members and five teaching assistants. We then discontinued the use of teaching assistants. We are convinced of the wisdom of that decision.

Graduate students are, of course, interesting and able young men and women. Many will soon be regular members of faculties and already at this stage of their careers display qualities that mark them as gifted teachers. But their situation, and their stage of development, precludes their general employment in lower-division "non-disciplinary" programs.

Graduate school is essentially a professional school, and a graduate student is preparing himself technically for entry into a profession. He can without too serious diversion from his primary task acquire some teaching experience as an assistant on a part-time basis. But this requires a carefully structured situation in which his developing technical competence can be used. To ask him to teach materials which lie outside his field makes very little sense. He should, at this stage, be immersed in his field, he is a young technician. If he is not, he will not be a graduate student very long.

The general use, and misuse, of teaching assistants in lower-division education is a major problem bordering on scandal. Limited technical use can be justified. But beyond that his use in free wheeling, lower-division programs is a disservice to student and teaching assistant alike. It is a temptation which must be strongly resisted.

III. *The American Year*

Two classes have gone through the first year of the program, and we have great confidence in its structure and value. The second, the "American" year, presents more complicated problems. It is not simply that the great books are not as obviously there. It is rather that we are more directly involved in and concerned with the *context* than we are during the first year. That is, our concern with America is different from our concern with Greece or England, which provided the setting for our study of general ideas. But America is the living society we now try to understand in the light of fundamental ideas which it embodies and issues which it faces. It is an oversimplification to say that we move from the general to the particular or from the abstract to the concrete or from the timeless to the temporal. But these contrasts suggest something of what is involved.

The curricular problem is a challenging one. There is, of course, American literature, American philosophy, American history to draw upon, but it would be a mistake to construct a second year which is simply a lesser and parochial version of the first year. Nor are we tempted, in our concern for the concrete and immediate, to fall into a "current events" curriculum.

We turn for salvation to the law and the court as the curricular basis of the second year—a solution which is itself characteristically American.

The Constitution has a place of special significance in American life. Seen as a "new covenant" it is an attempt to embody the moral and political experience of the old world in a framework appropriate for the new. The Supreme Court has produced a body of materials—interpretation, reflection, deliberation, argument, decision—of unusual educational fertility. This aspect of "law" has been badly neglected as a resource for general education, and it presents some difficulties. But to study the Supreme Court is to study the mind at work, attempting to deal with concrete and urgent problems in a context which demands justification in the light of laws, rules, principles, and purposes. Its failure and its triumphs, its confusions and its insights, its complexities and its simplicities are alike instructive. The Court is forced, by its unique position, to treat the particular in the light of the general, to square theory and practice—in short, to think about what we do.

We attempted, with some uncertainty and with mixed results, to make use of law as a teaching instrument in our first attempt at the second-year program. We will try again with greater confidence, determination, and experience.

We will not, of course, use constitutional and legal materials to the exclusion of everything else. But it will be the organizing focus of our work.

IV. *The Physical Setting*

Academic architecture presents us with the multipurpose office-classroom building on the one hand and the residence hall or dormitory on the other, and very little in between. The former is appropriate for the usual course-classroom mode of instruction and inadequate for anything beyond that. The residential center has its own peculiar shortcomings, but its possible use as a center of educational significance is a standing challenge.

Since some physical center is, we believe, essential to the development of educational programs, the conversion, and use, of the residence hall is worth consideration. If the Experimental Program is to be made permanent, and, perhaps, to expand, the question of its location in a dormitory cluster adjacent to the campus will have to be explored.

In the meantime we have had, in an abandoned fraternity house on the edge of the campus, an almost ideal home. It provides us with faculty offices, seminar rooms, study hall, and commons room. No one lives there, but it is available at all times for faculty and students in the program. Our reports in process have hinted that the house, in addition to its constructive significance, has been a more or less constant source of anxiety. It has been the island on which we have lived our own variations of the *Lord of the Flies*. It has provided a stage for the display of the roles of the guardian, the passive, the heedless, the predator. It has been the scene of both constructive and destructive energy.

Earlier hopes of Eden have been laid aside, and we now accept and value the house for what it is: a center of identification and of work, the sustainer of a common enterprise, and a laboratory which reveals to us all, faculty and students alike, the problems involved in the attempt to develop a community.

V. *Grades, Discipline, Drop-outs*

Choice of the pass–not pass option by students in the program is almost universal. Most requests for grades for a particular quarter are the result of a student's being placed on "probation" when, in his single outside course, he falls below a C. Of course, grades in the lower division are not as important as they are later in their bearing on admission to graduate or professional school, and we can provide special letters of recommendation for a variety of purposes. But the choice of the option, without serious faculty pressure, is a healthy sign. The faculty is very pleased with this solution to the grade problem and with the quality of analysis, discussion and criticism it makes possible.

Its chief value lies in its being not simply *another* grading system but in its not being a grading system at all. Thus, if we were to slide into a pass–not pass–distinction system, the whole point would be lost. There is a need for "not passed," but that comes close—as we have used it, and as we think it should be used—to "not performed."

The removal of grades affects us in two ways—and these effects must be recognized, and the needs, where legitimate, must be met somehow. First, grades are a traditional part of the incentive or motivation system; and second, they are the usual means by which students are, for various purposes, classified.

In our situation, the student and his work is well known to the faculty, and we can quite easily provide meaningful recommendations for scholarships, employment, transfer, and other purposes. We are not aware of any serious handicaps to our students on this score. But the elimination of grades does pose some marginal motivational, disciplinary, or "morale" problems. The problems are of a negative sort. That is, there is really no problem about most students, including the especially gifted ones. In spite of the fact that their experience has usually identified "doing good work" with "getting good grades" they adjust quickly to the new situation and thrive. They come to find satisfaction where it should be found in a book enjoyed and understood, in a clarifying discussion, in a piece of writing that makes sense, in an awareness of growing understanding and power. It is only when we are confronted with the inevitable forms of student delinquency that, reaching for the familiar instrument to evoke greater effort or to punish indolence or indifference, we find the holster empty. We can require attendance, we can require papers, we can try persuasion, but our only sanction is "not pass," which amounts to excommunication. And it is not easy to tell when this drastic action is called for.

We do not really consider the power to drop students from the program with a "not pass" for the quarter as a significant motivational influence. Work done simply to avoid that fate is not likely to be very useful. But we consider the "not pass" exclusion as necessary for the protection of the integrity of the program. The program consists of carefully scheduled prescribed work. Even in a "volunteer" student population there are some students who discover that they prefer to attend as they please, read what and as they please, and write what they please, if at all. *That* is not our program, and we do not intend to have it converted into that by students who opt for educational autonomy. When all else fails—and we do not wish to spoil the positive spirit of the program by constantly reacting to marginal delinquency—exclusion is necessary. It should be noted, however, that "not pass" exclusion has been resorted to rather rarely. Most students who, for one reason or another, become disaffected make their intention to leave the program known, complete the current quarter with somewhat diminishing performance, and depart in peace with a terminal "pass."

Our most irritating problem, however, is what to do about some fairly bright students who tend to have a high opinion of their own intellectual powers, who have learned to protect themselves against education, whose work is shoddy and disappointing, but who go through the motions sufficiently to retain their standing in the program. We are strongly tempted to exclude them, but so far we have not done so, although they are doing themselves little good, tend to demoralize their fellow students, and do not entertain the faculty.

APPENDIX

Plan of Program Given to Students at Start of Second Cycle, October 1967

The Program is an attempt to provide a coherent scheme of liberal education for the first two undergraduate years—a time during which the student is not yet pursuing a "major." The structure of the program is quite unlike the traditional one, but it has a structure of its own, which governs the educational life of its faculty and its students. It is not organized in terms of courses or academic subjects. It is, instead, based on a common, required curriculum—a program of reading, writing, and discussion.

The core of the program is a sequence of reading. The reading not only poses a number of persistent problems but serves as a focus for writing and discussion. In general, the readings themselves cluster about some periods in Western civilization during which a major crisis evokes a broad range of thoughtful and creative response. During the first year the focus is on Greece during the Peloponnesian wars and on seventeenth-century England. The second year focuses on America.

The Readings

The reading list is deceptively short. But we believe in reading a few great works in depth rather than reading a great many things in haste. The reading experience in the program is quite unlike what one has generally encountered in his earlier education. If, for example, we "read" the *Iliad* for a two-week period this is almost the equivalent, in time, of an entire quarter course. But the work is concentrated and undistracted since, generally, we are reading only one thing at a time. Thus, one can read the *Iliad*, in a preliminary way, in several days; but that reading only scratches the surface, and we must learn how to get beyond that with the aid of discussion, writing, rereading and rereading.

Generally, we do not require or even advise the reading of secondary works or scholarly commentary, although students may, of course, do so if they have time. While two weeks may, at the outset, seem to be a long time to spend on the *Iliad*, the time will, at the end, seem all too short. If we are working properly, every book will be laid aside with regret.

Writing

We approach writing with the conviction that a student can hardly do too much of it. The program policy is that the student should write every day for the entire two-year period. The theory is not that we are out to produce "writers," but that writing as a habitual exercise calls on us to develop clarity, coherence, and other powers of analysis and expression, and contributes to our capacity to read perceptively and to engage in fruitful discussion.

The writing program will normally be coordinated with the reading and will involve:

(1) Formal papers—about five each quarter—on topics and in a form to be assigned by the faculty.

(2) A log or journal in which each student is to write every day. This should be a page or two which develops some idea raised by the reading or in seminar or lecture. The log is to be available for faculty scrutiny on appropriate occasions.

Discussion

Students, in seminar groups of eight, will meet twice each week —once with a faculty member present and once without. The discussion is to be focused on the questions or problems raised by the reading. Discussion is a difficult art with a complex moral and intellectual structure. It involves listening and responding as well as speaking. It calls for judgment about significance and relevance, and it requires adequate preparation. The seminars can be a stimulating and exciting aspect of the program.

Lectures

Twice a week (Tuesday and Thursday, 10-12) the student body and faculty assemble for something like a general lecture-discussion session. Sometimes a faculty member may deliver a lecture or speak for a half hour or more. On other occasions a number of faculty members may have a panel discussion. There will usually be questions from students, and responses. Sometimes we will have a guest lecturer.

Again, the "lectures" will be related to the reading. The purpose is not to give background information or to explain the reading but rather to deepen the issues, to offer suggestive interpretations, and generally to spark consideration of fundamental problems.

Conferences

Each student will have a different faculty member as his seminar leader or instructor each quarter. The instructor will read and comment on the papers and may, from time to time, hold individual conferences. These conferences may occur either on the initiative of the instructor or of the student—as needed rather than on a regularly scheduled basis.

Informal Activity

The house, which has been assigned to the program for its exclusive use, is the physical center for most of our activity. Faculty offices are located there, and seminars are held there. But, in addition, it is available for a wide range of informal uses by members of the program. Coffee is available at all hours, the lounge is pleasant and convenient for conversation, and a quiet reading room is available.

It is hoped that the house will be used by the students for a variety of appropriate informal activities—morning, afternoon, and evening.

It should be noted that the general resources of the University are available for students in the Program—libraries, gymnasia and sport facilities, lectures, concerts—and it is expected that our students will live fairly active lives.

The "Subject"

Since we do not organize our work in terms of such familiar fields or disciplines as economics, sociology, political science, history, or literature, it is difficult to give a simple answer to the question, "But what are you studying?" Nor is it quite accurate to say that the program is "interdisciplinary." We are concerned with certain fundamental human problems, although it would seem pretentious to say that we are studying the problems of freedom, order, justice, authority, conscience, war, rebellion, and tyranny. But these, among others, are problems with which the Greeks struggled; they are problems which dominate the mind and spirit of seventeenth-century England; they constitute, in some mysterious sense, the American agenda; they are problems we grapple with as we try to create a significant life in this time and this place. This, as we see it, is the "subject" of liberal education; this is what the reading is about.

Some General Observations

Of course, formal assignments or activities, crucial as they are, constitute only a minimal aspect of education. They are the necessary ceremony or ritual which aid in the development of the appropriate habit or cast of mind. They are to be taken religiously—that is, seriously—but for anyone in search of education they do not define the limits of his work. The student is the ultimate steward of his energies; the institution can guide, encourage, advise, and sustain. But it cannot simply *give* him his education.

The program frees the student from many of the prods and checks to which he has become accustomed. There are no examinations; the pass–not pass system can remove much of the competitive grade pressure; the small number of formal "classes" gives him a great deal of unscheduled time. He will have to learn to use his time and energy fruitfully in an environment full of random excitement, enticement, and distraction.

To enroll in the program is to assume certain commitments. It is to become one of a group seeking to create a learning community, to engage in a common intellectual life. Education is not entirely a private matter; it is a social enterprise. And it has its obligations. Thus, for example, every student is expected—required—to attend every formally scheduled meeting, lecture, or seminar; to do the reading carefully and thoroughly, to turn in promptly papers which represent his best efforts. The freedom which we cultivate is the freedom of mastery, not of impulse.

Calendar for First Year, Readings
(Three 10-Week Quarters)

Fall Quarter

1. Homer's *Iliad*
2. *Iliad*
3. Homer's *Odyssey*; Xenephon's *Anabasis*; Hesiod's *Works and Days*
4. Thucydides' *Peloponnesian War* ⎫
5. *Peloponnesian War*   ⎬ Supplemented by selected lives from Plutarch and comedies by Aristophanes
6. *Peloponnesian War*   ⎭
7. Aeschylus' *Oresteia*
8. Sophocles' Three Theban Plays
9. Euripides' *The Bacchae*
10. Plato's *Apology* and *Crito*

Winter Quarter

1. Plato's *Gorgias*
2. Plato's *Republic*
3. *Republic*

4. *Republic*
5. Bible ⎫
6. Bible ⎬ Selections from the King James version
7. Bible ⎭
8. Shakespeare's *King Lear*
9. Machiavelli's *The Prince*
10. (Short Quarter)

Spring Quarter

1. Milton's *Paradise Lost*
2. *Paradise Lost*
3. Hobbes's *Leviathan*
4. *Leviathan*
5. *Leviathan*
6. J. S. Mill's *On Liberty*
7. *On Liberty*
8. Arnold's *Culture and Anarchy*
9. *Culture and Anarchy*
10. General Review

Readings for Second Year

(This list is tentative, and probably incomplete. The sequence is subject to change.)

Fall Quarter

Henry Adams   *The U.S. in 1880*
The Flag Salute Cases   U.S. Supreme Court
The Federalist Papers and The Constitution

McCulloch v. Maryland	(John Marshall)
Calhoun	*Disquisitions on Government*
Edmund Burke	*Selections*

Winter Quarter

Supreme Court cases on church & state, conscience, freedom.
Thoreau (selections)
Meiklejohn   *Political Freedom*

Spring Quarter

Marx (selections)
Freud (selected works)
The Education of Henry Adams
The Autobiography of Lincoln Steffens
The Autobiography of Malcolm X
Meiklejohn   *Education Between Two Worlds*